1970
Maximum Muscle

The
Pinnacle of
Muscle Car
Power

Mark Fletcher & Richard Truesdell

motorbooks

Contents

___Introduction

GIMME DANGER

As the 1960s roared to a close, rapid changes were happening in popular culture. As one example, music created specifically for youth—legendary artists such as Elvis, Chubby Checker ("The Twist"), the Beach Boys ("I Get Around"), and the Beatles—morphed into more *aggressive* hard-rock sounds from bands such as Led Zeppelin and, in Detroit, the Stooges and the politically charged MC5.

When the space race reached its zenith with Neil Armstrong's first dusty footsteps on the Moon's surface on July 21, 1969, the Vietnam War and draft lottery still loomed over the heads of young Americans. Youth rioted in the streets to protest the government's sacrifice of Americans in a war they argued had no possible honorable outcome, but also in reaction to worsening race relations. To many, the Woodstock festival in August 1969 stands as the ultimate symbol of the period's reactionary antiestablishment, with its open displays of sex, drugs, and rock and roll. Arguably, however, the Rolling Stones' own disastrous music festival, at Altamont Speedway in northern California—during the final month of the decade, no less—was the real embodiment of the zeitgeist.

The younger generation had always been on a different page than that of its parents, but the chasm was widening noticeably. It was not uncommon to see young folks dressed in robes holding signs declaring, *The End Is Near*, but the question was, "The end of what?" The war? Our youth? The world? It seemed society was accelerating, but in what direction?

⬆ Commander Neil Armstrong took this photo of Buzz Aldrin as the two Americans walked on the Moon July 20th, 1969 fulfilling Kennedy's challenge to accomplish the task by the end of the decade. ⬈ The fast-paced decade of the 1960s saw a rise in American civil unrest.

⬆ The 1964 Pontiac GTO is considered by many to be the first muscle car. The large-displacement 389-cubic-inch engine that was traditionally found in full-size cars was first offered in a midsize sedan and created a unique power-to-weight ratio advantage. This is the actual car tested by *Car and Driver*'s infamous March 1964 issue when it was compared to a Ferrari GTO.

WHY 1970?

In Detroit, society's acceleration was paralleled by automotive engineers and their steady development of horsepower. What had started in the late 1950s as a war of chrome and fins had, by the late 1960s, escalated into a horsepower battle among the four domestic manufacturers. The 1957 full-size Chevrolet had been advertised with a sensational 1 horsepower per cubic inch. Although that meant the 283-cubic-inch V-8 with fuel injection produced an impressive 283 horsepower, it had to move around 3,283 pounds of iron and fell short of what would later be considered a benchmark: 10 pounds per horsepower. (The classic definition of what would later be considered a muscle car was the biggest engine possible installed in the engine bay of an intermediate- or smaller-sized car as best exemplified by Pontiac's 1964 Tempest GTO: a 3,106-pound car with 325 advertised horsepower, just under the magical 10 pounds per horsepower benchmark.)

Other GM divisions, as well as Chrysler and Ford, responded. And with the April 1964 introduction of the Mustang, it was just a matter of time—until 1967, to be exact—before big-block engines would find their way under the hoods of what were essentially compact cars.

This book's genesis was a discussion among a group of enthusiasts about what the ultimate muscle-car collection should include. The compiled list almost exclusively comprised cars manufactured during an eighteen-month period: most automotive aficionados will agree the best of the best were built from midyear 1969 to the final days of the 1970 model year.

You could accurately argue that rarer cars were built both before and after this brief timeframe, but history shows that the period saw the release of a frenzy of marketing specials and formidable street warriors while the situation was still favorable for sales.

Why did Detroit release so many midyear 1969 cars and then one-up themselves with the ultimate high-performance cars released for the strike-shortened 1970 model year? The origins of this vast assortment of power were also a large reason for its quick demise. Two significant factors developing completely separately of each other would combine in the fatal blow to the muscle car market.

CALIFORNIA KILLED THE MUSCLE CAR

The term *smog* was commonly used in California in the 1940s to describe a combination of smoke from industries and naturally occurring fog. By midcentury, smog was a daily occurrence in Los Angeles and was even occasionally mistaken for enemy gas attacks during World War II. By the early 1950s it was clear that the emissions from transportation sources were the leading culprits in the growing smog problem, not just in the greater Los Angeles area but in most major cities. The frequency and intensity of the smog prodded municipalities to form the South Coast Air Quality Management District in 1953, directed toward manufacturing emissions and the region's growing numbers of automobiles.

By 1959 the counties were having difficulty regulating air quality, and the state legislature developed the California Motor Vehicle Pollution Control Board (CMVPCB), giving it the authority to test and certify emission-control systems. One of the first requirements it established resulted in the addition of closed-crankcase ventilation systems. The positive crankcase ventilation (PCV) valve was ordered added to all new automobiles sold in California beginning in 1963. Manufacturers easily converted new models to this system, and the first emission-control devices were included with all new cars sold in North America.

According to Caltech professor Arie Haagen-Smit, who analyzed the composition of smog, one-third of airborne contaminates were created by automobiles in the form of hydrocarbons or unburnt gas. It wasn't long until the California board was asking for more stringent controls. In 1960 University of California Los Angeles engineers Richard Kopa and Hiroshi Kimura tested the first automotive catalytic converter device that cut nitrogen oxide tailpipe emissions by 50 percent. They tested it on a 1959 Ford wagon driven in and around the greater Los Angeles area a full fifteen years before catalytic converters would become standard equipment on all new US cars.

In 1966 California formed the Bureau of Air Sanitation, which became the California Air Resources Board (CARB) in 1967. New cars sold in Southern California included an air pump system that injected atmospheric oxygen into the exhaust side of the combustion chambers. This oxygen, when combined with the heated exhaust gases, burned excess fuel that would otherwise be dumped into the atmosphere through the tailpipe.

At the same time the federal government was forming the Motor Vehicle Air Pollution Control Act of 1965, which required all cars sold in the United States beginning in 1968 to meet stringent air-quality tests conducted by the manufacturer and based primarily on the research done on behalf of California. This act did not require the owner to maintain or test the systems, although California soon enacted legislation to hold the vehicle owner responsible for this function. These standards enabled new car exhaust emission reductions of 72 percent for hydrocarbons, 56 percent for carbon monoxide, and 100 percent for crankcase hydrocarbons.

⬆ By the early 1970s, air pollution visibly shrouded the streets of Southern California on a daily basis. ⬈ The first installation of a catalytic converter was tested on a 1959 Ford Ranch Wagon.

California's climate and topography, combined with its large automobile population and the high number of miles driven by Southern Californians, resulted in the state having the worst air quality in the nation. Under the federally assigned autonomous authority, CARB would go on to institute the nation's first nitrogen oxide (NOx) emissions standards for motor vehicles and led the way to the development of the catalytic converter that would revolutionize the reduction of smog-forming emissions from cars.

In 1970 the Environmental Protection Agency (EPA) was created through executive order by President Richard Nixon. Although the agency concerned itself with all contaminates impacting the safety of the Americans, it concentrated its efforts on air pollution. Additionally the federal Clean Air Act of the same year required stringent emission controls to be installed in all new cars sold in North America by 1976. These new federal requirements were incompatible with the high-compression motors being designed by powertrain engineers in Detroit, who would need to turn their attention to emissions and fuel efficiency.

CRASHING CARS
CRASH MUSCLE-CAR SALES

Military veterans returning from Vietnam were crucial to triggering the muscle-car era. Along with the manufacturers producing ever more powerful cars, vets were key players in the perfect storm.

Those returning had both the money and the desire to buy Detroit's new generation of high-powered cars. Having survived the horrific experience of war, returning to a level of normalcy was first on their agenda. Some took advantage of post exchange (PX) discounts that enabled them to order cars prior to returning stateside. Paul Heller was one such veteran. His on-base PX exchange in South Vietnam offered him the opportunity to order a brand-new 1968 Chevrolet Nova. As he looked through the catalog at the PX, his eyes fell on a page with a picture of the newly released AMC Javelin. He studied the ad and then ordered his car to be delivered to his local AMC dealer in Southern California so it would be waiting for him when he returned home. (Like many of his fellow veterans, within two years he was forced to trade in the Javelin in exchange for keeping his driver's license. The "suggestion" came from the local judge who was tired of seeing him in court.)

The combination of testosterone and increased horsepower caused insurance companies to make higher payouts. Automotive insurance in 1965 averaged $30 per month for young drivers regardless of gender, but insurance companies began tracking the high-risk factors that were leading to their lower profits. Actuaries determined that the industry's sharp rise in payouts correlated with horsepower ratings, and by the beginning of 1969 they had developed a hit list of popular models that incurred higher premiums for young drivers. It was not uncommon for the cost of insurance to equal or even exceed the monthly finance payments of a new car. Typically a driver under twenty-five considering purchase of a new Chevelle Super Sport for $130 a month would find their insurance payment quoted at $100 a month—a combined total equivalent to almost $1,700 in 2020 dollars. Opting for the more sedate Malibu two-door hardtop with the optional 350-cubic-inch V-8, automatic transmission, and bucket seats would cut their insurance cost by more than half.

By quickly releasing special-package performance cars with new model names, manufacturers hoped to stay ahead of the insurance adjusters' curated lists of high-performance cars. Like a tethered Cox toy airplane that sped up as it ran out of gas, the muscle-car industry accelerated at top speed prior to 1970—then rather quickly ended by mid-decade. (The 1973 OPEC oil embargo didn't help, as the midsize market segment transitioned from performance to luxury.)

DETROIT RESPONDS TO
THE SMALL-CAR INVASION

Emissions controls and legislation and skyrocketing insurance costs were not the only predictors of the muscle car's downfall. The impending introduction of small cars fed into the end of the muscle-car era as well. New-car announcements for the 1970 and 1971 model years included affordable domestic subcompacts whose rise would coincide directly with the fall of the muscle car.

The end of this era was not unexpected. As early as 1967 design teams at AMC, Ford, and GM had been pulled aside to develop small-displacement engines for subcompacts designed to go head to head with Volkswagen and with cars coming from Japan in increasing volume. (Chrysler would take a different approach, which will be explained later.) These new four-cylinder engine designs were influenced directly by the Japanese and European markets.

Previously, overseas competitors had not been part of the American car manufacturers' product development plans. A new entry into the US market in the late 1950s, Volkswagen had a paltry 2 percent market share in the early 1960s. By the 1968 model year, VW had grown to an almost 5 percent share of all cars sold in North America. This did not go unnoticed. By 1968 each of the Big Three had their own secret small-car program in full swing. Previously, Chevrolet had offered the low-price two-door Corvair 500 as a competitor to the Volkswagen Beetle. However, Ralph Nader's 1965 book *Unsafe at Any Speed*—which demonstrated the first-generation 1960–1963 Corvair rear-axle design to be unpredictable at its handling limits—and the success of the Ford Mustang would be the nails in the Corvair's coffin.

Chevrolet's next answer to the growing sales of imports was the small and sporty Vega with its ill-fated four-cylinder aluminum engine. Product design started in the summer of 1968 with GM chief engineer Ed Cole promising an import beater within twenty-four months at a press event reminiscent of John F. Kennedy's declaration to land a man on the Moon by the end of the decade. JFK's promise was fulfilled on July 20, 1969; the Vega was introduced less than one year later, on June 26, 1970, as a 1971 model.

In 1968 and 1969 AMC also took on Volkswagen with a stripped-down version of the existing Rambler American. It sold for $1,839, less than $200 more than the port-of-entry price of the hot-selling Volkswagen Beetle. AMC stressed the Rambler's more powerful six-cylinder engine and seating for six adults. One very creative ad showed a Rambler with an upside-down Beetle strapped to its roof. In reality, the Rambler became a stopgap measure similar to the Corvair.

The Gremlin was the first of the domestic subcompacts designed specifically to take on the imports. Developed concurrently with the all-new 1970 Hornet by the always cash-strapped AMC, it released on April Fool's Day 1970 as a midyear model that shared sheet metal with the two-door Hornet from the B-pillar forward as a cost-saving measure. Available in two- and four-passenger versions ($1,879 and $1,959, respectively), it was AMC's low-price leader, just a couple hundred dollars more than the class-leading Beetle.

At Ford, the compact-sized Maverick, introduced in the late 1960s, was the automaker's first attempt to compete with the Beetle. Like AMC's repositioning of the low-priced Rambler, the Maverick enjoyed success against the Volkswagen, but it was not a true subcompact (rather, it was based on the Falcon platform introduced in 1960).

Ford's real entry into the subcompact arena came via the Pinto. Initial planning was for a 2,000-pound car for under $2,000. Like the other domestic manufacturers, Ford was aware it needed a subcompact quickly to stop the sales erosion

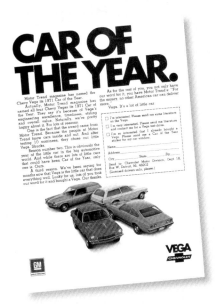

← By 1971 the new car market had shifted to a more practical and economic approach. Small-car production quickly outpaced the performance models. Muscle cars were a victim to changing tastes. ↓ Each domestic manufacturer introduced their version of a small car for the masses. American Motors introduced the Gremlin on April 1, 1970, in both four-passenger and a price-leader two-passenger version that did not include a back seat.

the imports were creating, especially with young buyers. Ford president Lee Iacocca tasked engineers with bringing the car to market in a short twenty-five-month window (compared to the industry average of forty-three months). This resulted in a miniaturized version of other Ford products, which stifled any creative innovations. Further, the rush to production led to some design and cost compromises, above all the exploding gas tanks that ultimately doomed the Pinto and landed it on many "Worst Cars of All Time" lists.

Chrysler lagged behind the other American manufacturers in the race to develop competitors to the imports. Caught without a plan for a subcompact, Dodge turned to Japan, partnering with Mitsubishi in 1969 to "Americanize" its Galant to meet the upcoming more stringent federal requirements.

Meanwhile, Chrysler's Plymouth brand turned to its British subsidiary, the Rootes Group (Sunbeam), and Americanized its existing Hillman Avenger, a very conventional front-engine, rear-wheel-drive four-door subcompact now dubbed the Cricket. So typical of British cars of that era, the Cricket suffered from lax quality control and lasted only until 1973, with fewer than fifty thousand sold. These two cars allowed Chrysler to field subcompacts quickly, but neither enjoyed the sales success of the Pinto, the Vega, or even the Gremlin.

⬆ Chevrolet used this iconic photo to introduce what some consider to be the ultimate muscle car, the LS6 454-powered 1970 Chevelle SS rated at 450 horsepower.

DOING WHAT THEY DO BEST: MUSCLE CARS

The American manufacturers' new subcompact programs were going on during the height of the muscle-car wars among the domestic automakers. But each had limited resources, and by the end of the decade, much of their engineering talent had been transferred to the small-car programs and to initiatives to meet upcoming emission and safety standards. All four domestic manufacturers could see the writing on the wall, so they worked at warp speed to get their muscle cars released, accelerating the programs for introduction midyear 1969, and then pulled out all the stops for their peak muscle cars for the 1970 model year.

On the marketing side, personnel also knew the shift was imminent and that they had a brief eighteen-month window to capitalize on the performance buyers' available income. Rising insurance rates meant fewer sales or lower-optioned vehicles, either of which meant a smaller profit.

Despite the introduction of several great muscle cars for 1968 through 1970, sales remained steady. Another consideration that affected sales in 1970 was the UAW strikes that devastated General Motors for that year.

➡ Although many reflect on the Pinto as a disposable car, it was an extremely successful product line to Ford: a smaller, simpler car that cost the consumer about half the price of the average muscle car. Millions were sold within the first few years of production and spawned the introduction of the subcompact Mustang II for the 1974 model year.

to Mayhem

JAMMIN' ECONO:
The Low-Cost Drag Cars

AMC Hurst SC/Rambler

Plymouth Road Runner and Dodge Super Bee A12

Pontiac GTO "The Judge"

Mercury Cougar Eliminator

In 1969 two entities sanctioned professional drag racing in the United States: the National Hot Rod Association (NHRA) and the American Hot Rod Association (AHRA). The organizations set the rules and provided the means by which cars ran and championships were awarded in their various divisions. Much of this administration was regional in nature.

Particular cars and engine options were assigned to stock classes based on calculated—not advertised—horsepower, along with each vehicle's track weight. To compete in a stock class, a car could have only factory-original parts complete with part number documentation. Fitting aftermarket performance parts bumped the average racer into the modified classes, a far more competitive and expensive field to play in.

Not all factory parts were created equal, however. To offer their customers some extra punch, major carmakers—original equipment manufacturers (OEMs)—had been making more capable components available as aftermarket parts in their factory production parts books. These goodies were available at the parts counters of many dealerships, which would help their customers find higher performance while allowing them to remain in the stock classes. By 1969 the Big Three and American Motors were offering specific models fitted by the factory, or an authorized subcontractor, with the otherwise aftermarket parts. This approach allowed those models to escape controversy during tech inspections concerning whether any of its parts qualified as factory stock.

Perhaps because they were focused on components, OEMs sometimes underestimated their performance cars' horsepower or overestimated their curb weight. These innocent oversights created advantages when those models were matched to classes at the track. Luckily for the competition, the sanctioning bodies would notice these "mistakes" based on track results, recalculate overperforming cars' horsepower, and often bump them into more difficult classes midseason.

By 1969 the many special-production cars released by OEMs in limited numbers were dominating the national drag-racing scene. Cars such as the 1968½ Mustang with a 428 Cobra Jet engine were distributed among top drivers and successfully campaigned across the nation. Fans and the media took notice, bringing their admiration and checkbooks to the dealerships. For the auto industry, it was a time of "Win on Sunday, sell on Monday."

It was also for 1969 that the sanctioning bodies raised the minimum production numbers factories would have to hit in order for a car to qualify in one of the stock classes. Instead of the prior approach of creating a special production run of, say, 50 cars that would be driven at the national level by professionals, automakers were now required to produce 500 to 1,500 units of a model and distribute it through established dealer networks.

The new rules didn't dissuade OEMs from the weekend drag-race scene that was showcasing their vehicles. Five worthy offerings released as midyear 1969 cars and priced within reach of the determined low-budget quarter-miler were AMC's Hurst SC/Rambler, Dodge's Super Bee A12, Plymouth's Road Runner A12, Pontiac's GTO "Judge," and the mid-year Mercury Cougar Eliminator package.

All of these offerings had a common thread of performance, image, and affordability. Most postproduction evaluations reflect that the manufacturers succeeded in improving their products' performance images with these packages, although that victory provided little or no improvement to the corporate bottom line.

EVEN AS LATE AS 1969, a portion of the motoring public still said "Nash" to refer to American Motors Corporation. But AMC had been evolving, starting with a management shakeup in 1967. A new board of directors was looking to lose the stodgy image created by the company's reliable and economical Ramblers. They charted a new course, hoping to attract the substantial market of baby boomers who were soon maturing to a driving age.

AMC leadership gambled, as did those in charge at the Big Three, that what moved fast at the track would move fast from the showroom. The carmaker's new model name was a frank embodiment of its objective—a sharp-nosed projectile hurled through the air with maximum force at track-and-field events. The Javelin appeared in fall 1967 for the '68 model year. The four-seat pony car was designed to compete with Ford's Mustang and Mercury Cougar, GM's Chevrolet Camaro and Pontiac Firebird, and Chrysler's Plymouth Barracuda. AMC followed with the Javelin-based two-seat AMX in early 1968. Concurrently, the company introduced the biggest engine in its history: a healthy 390-cubic-inch V-8 to supplement its small-block 290- and 343-cubic-inch V-8s. The new metal and muscle caught the public's attention.

A year later, in late winter 1969, AMC put its foot to the floor with the Hurst SC/Rambler, based on the Rambler Rogue hardtop. The new model's bold red, white, and blue paint declared AMC's place in the center of the American muscle-car market. Between the start of 1968 and the end of 1969, the company launched seven major racing projects to demonstrate the prowess of its new, more youthful lineup of performance-oriented cars.

American Motors' advertising agency, Wells Rich Greene, was tuned in to the youth market. Its television and aggressive print ads reflected a polite anti-adult slant that was humorous to younger buyers as well as their parents. Two unknown yet clever advertising writers, Charles Moss and Stan Dragoti (who was married to actress

⬆ The SC/Rambler hood scoop is a predominant feature. Although extremely functional, it has been described as looking similar to a drive-up mailbox.

⬇ This dealer handout outlines the Hurst-designed SC/Rambler specifications in an unusual three-color print.

➡➡ There were two paint schemes for the 1969 AMC SC/Rambler: the more common A-Scheme with full Matador Red sides and the more subtle B-Scheme with thin blue and red stripes low on each side. Only 292 B-Scheme were made out of the 1512 SC/Ramblers produced.

➥➥ The redline tires were a common performance-car option in the 1960s. By 1970 the white letter tire replaced the redline tire for most car offerings.

⬇ Based on a low-cost sedan with off-the-shelf components used by AMC on their Javelin and AMX, the SC/Rambler was a unique offering in 1969 as most special package cars were based on the new pony car models.

Cheryl Tiegs from 1970 to 1979 and had a degree of success as a Hollywood writer and director), penned a new ad campaign. Neither was a traditional car guy, but both understood that AMC needed to leave the stodgy Rambler behind with the smoke of burning rubber.

Ads for the flamboyant Hurst SC/Rambler hit the pages of *Hot Rod* magazine in March 1969 to serve one purpose: drive young buyers in every city, town, and hamlet into the nearest AMC dealership. AMC even sent a letter to dealers telling them to display the Hurst SC/Rambler in a corner window and to make sure to have plenty of the more practical (and profitable) Javelins and sporty Rebels available for the influx of young buyers. The tactic was successful. Javelins sales grew from 1968 to 1969.

The *Hot Rod* ad featured both the car's price ($2,998) and its quarter-mile time (14.3 seconds). No other OEM car ad had ever called out a model's elapsed time for the quarter mile. This data was not meant just to sell cars—it was an out-and-out challenge to the Big Three. Their response would be swift: "Challenge accepted!"

SC stood for Super Coupe, a name backed up by the best go-quick goodies AMC could fit from its parts shelf. The body was derived from a standard two-door Rogue hardtop, which had been stripped of most bodyside adornments. Fender lips were rolled to accommodate bolder Firestone F70-14 bias-ply redline tires wrapped around Bright Blue Magnum 500–style steel wheels. American-flag colors emerged from an Appliance White body embellished with touches of bright red and blue. The more common A-Scheme paint featured bright red sides and a wide blue stripe down the top. The rarer B-Scheme was all white topside with a narrow red stripe down the sides crossing the fender wells, a line of white beneath it, and a broader blue band dressing the bottom edge. The hood boasted a boy-racer scoop raised 8 inches over stock and lunged forward with a mail slot–style opening. To coach any air that might otherwise escape the intake manifold, graphics pointed the way to the scoop with a bright blue arrow. Matching white-painted racing mirrors promoted this apex Rambler's go, along with three SC/Hurst emblems—one on each front fender and another next to the blacked-out taillight panel on the passenger side so that your street competitor could explain what had just beat him.

Drivers who lost a sprint to this machine could take at least a little satisfaction from seeing a rare beast in the wild; the SC/Rambler registry indicates that 1,220 examples were built with A-Scheme paint and 292 in B-Scheme dress.

Inside, the Hurst SC retained the Rogue-emblemed door panels and comfortable, fully reclining split bench seats but finished in a drab taxicab Charcoal Gray vinyl trim. The dash featured a chromed Rogue gauge bezel and three-spoke wood-grained steering wheel with a Sun ST-635 tachometer fixed to the steering column—just like they used at the races. Jutting from the floor was a chrome Hurst shifter with the infamous T-Handle connected to a Borg Warner T-10 transmission with the 2.23:1 first gear used in all AMC manuals in 1969.

Underneath the hood scoop was a factory-stock 390-cubic-inch V-8 with 425 foot-pounds of torque transplanted directly from the 1969 AMX. The only difference was an open-element air-cleaner lid in place of the AMX's sealed top unit. This was coupled to a fiberglass tub that fit inside the factory air-cleaner housing and sealed to the hood with a vacuum-controlled ram-air valve that opened during hard acceleration to increase the cool air captured by that massive scoop. This ram-air feature added an estimated 10 to 15 horsepower, though AMC chose to go with the standard rating of 315 horsepower.

A studious AMC'er may know that a heater valve in the intake manifold indicates a Javelin or AMX motor. The valve would not fit in the smaller Rambler American engine bay and was replaced with a simple heater hose fitting on the SC/Rambler's hefty 390.

Additional drivetrain upgrades included heavy-duty suspension with power front disc brakes and larger rear drum brakes than found on other Rogues. The rear had the AMC 20 Twin-Grip differential with 3.54:1 final ratio. Factory-installed torque links taken directly from the 1969 AMX reduced wheel hop under hard acceleration. Steering was accomplished through a manual steering box with a 16:1 quick ratio.

⬆ All 1,512 SC/Ramblers were identically equipped from the factory. This car dealer added bumper guards and AM radio. Only 292 received the more subtle B-Scheme paint treatment.

The total Hurst SC/Rambler package was advertised at a mere $2,998 plus destination charges. It was, to put it mildly, a performance-car bargain of the first order. A comparably equipped Rogue hardtop with the smaller 290-cubic-inch V-8, four-speed transmission, Twin-Grip rear, front disc brakes, and other performance upgrades (if available) cost $850 *more*.

The car was designed to compete in the NHRA's F-Stock class, one of various divisions established by a factor of horsepower to weight. The sweet spot for the little AMC was the 10-pounds-per-horsepower ratio. With an advertised 315 horsepower, the car needed to weigh in at over 3,150 pounds to make the class. AMC finessed the numbers, generously stating curb weight at 3,160 pounds against the alleged power figure, which overlooked more than a few horses.

The original plan to build only 500 units was quickly expanded to 1,500 when orders through its roughly 1,700 dealers were higher than expected. AMC also wanted to use up more of the 1969 390 engines because of a casting design change for the 1970 model year.

The SC/Rambler was a true all-in-one, drive-off-the-showroom-floor package. There were no factory-installed options. All cars were identical apart from the two paint schemes, with no deviations or additions. Even the radio was a dealer-installed option. The cars were assembled on the AMC East production line along with all other Rambler Americans, Javelins, and AMXs. Hurst received $200 per car for designing the package and providing the SC/Hurst emblems, bullet-style mirrors, hood scoop, fiberglass air-cleaner tub, Hurst shifter, Thrush mufflers, Sun tach, and stripe kit. Hurst paid brush ace Paul Hatton to travel to the Kenosha plant each weekend to hand-pinstripe around the red billboard sides on each A-Scheme car.

The SC/Rambler was a track success, consistently dipping into the high 13s with no alterations from stock other than a performance tune and a pair of cheater slicks. Its high-profile appearance also succeeded in making it an easy-to-spot streetlight dominator.

⬆⬆ The 1969 SC/Rambler was anything but subtle. Both the factory Thrush glass pack mufflers and the red, white, and blue paint were in-your-face.

⬆ The SC/Rambler utilized the standard AMX 390 engine and carried over the same emblem.

⬅ The SC/Rambler was a well-balanced muscle car able to traverse the quarter mile in 14.3 seconds in factory trim. Its biggest drawback was lack of traction due to the rear wheel well design that limited the size of tire that could be installed.

Plymouth Road Runner and Dodge Super Bee A12

PLYMOUTH'S ROAD RUNNER hit the scene in September 1967 as a 1968 model, following the basic hot-rod guidebook with pared-down body and trim and hurled by a stout V-8. Based on the newly redesigned midsize B-body intermediate on a 116-inch wheelbase, the car in standard guise cradled Chrysler's 383 Wedge engine. With its stock four-barrel, this 335-horsepower V-8 moved a car with total weight of 3,436 pounds. First-year sales were brisk, built on solid dollar value for a high-performance midsize package.

The Road Runner found a ready market eager to trade dollars for horsepower. Within it was a small subset of drivers willing to pay a lot of dollars for a lot of power. Plymouth had them covered too. Those who checked off the box for the 426-cubic-inch Hemi engine entered the top tier of the muscle-car hierarchy and quickly became leaders of the pack. The price was steep, though—$813 to be exact (with "mandatory" options). And all that juice underfoot made the car high-strung for a daily driver. Only 798 customers ordered the Hemi option for 1969.

If there was something vaguely absurd about building street-legal hot rods for everyday motorists, both sides of the transaction were in on the gag. This was, after all, a model named after an animated bird. Plymouth paid Warner Bros. $50,000 for the rights to the Road Runner cartoon character. They even created a "beep beep" horn, painted purple to stand out from other components in the engine bay.

Plymouth's sibling, Dodge, also got in on the fun with the similarly configured Super Bee. Derived from the Coronet, the Super Bee wheelbase was 1 inch longer and slightly heavier. Like its bird brother, the Dodge was introduced with the 383 Wedge V-8 as standard, plus the Hemi option for those with dollars but no time to spare. The cars in showroom trim with the more common engine could eat up the quarter mile in a respectable 14.4 seconds.

⬇ This Plymouth Road Runner is equipped with the A12 package, meaning it featured the big-block 440 with three two-barrel carbs.

One group enjoying the speed craze less than the carmakers and drivers was the insurance industry. These sourpusses with their actuaries and loss data were casting a bit of a shadow over the performance party across manufacturers. Because premiums were a budget factor that consumers had to reckon with, manufacturers had to deal with them too.

By releasing performance-enhanced models midyear, automakers hoped to get less scrutiny from underwriters. For this reason, the Road Runner and Super Bee A12, Boss Mustang, Superbird, Daytona, Talladega, Trans Am, and others were all released in mid-year 1969.

Ideally for Plymouth and Dodge, all of their prospective customers and none of their insurers would receive the March 1969 issue of *Hot Rod* magazine. That was the edition introducing the midyear 1969 Super Bee and Road Runner, now available with the A12 option—a 440-cubic-inch V-8 with three two-barrel carbs feeding a cast-aluminum Edelbrock intake manifold. Topped off with a special oval ram-air air cleaner that mated to the fiberglass hood, the Six Pack V-8 option provided a rated 390 horsepower.

Intrigued, *Drag Racing* put Buddy Martin behind the wheel of a Vitamin C Orange A12 Super Bee weighing in at 3,765 pounds including driver and a tank of gas. As reported in the magazine's June 1969 issue, Martin threw the Dodge down the quarter mile in 12.98 seconds, reaching 111 miles per hour.

The 440 Six Pack engine was not simply a 440 Magnum with three two-barrel carbs stuck on top. To produce the factory-stated 390 horsepower at 4,700 rpm, it featured special 10.1:1 compression-ratio pistons, heavy-duty rods, and a combination of 440 and 426 Hemi internal components yielding a massive 490 foot-pounds of torque at 3,600 rpm. Vacuum progression allowed the big mill to run on the single, central

↑ This 1969 Super Bee sports aftermarket Cragar five-spoke wheels. Most performance cars were swiftly personalized with aftermarket components when new.

⬆ Using a base-model two-door sedan, this A12 Road Runner sported minimal trim. Unsuspecting street racers might have been tipped off by the lack of hub caps, which exposed its lug nuts.

two-barrel rated at 350 cfm for light town cruising, then engage the larger 500-cfm units at either end with a stomp on the go pedal when it was time to blur scenery.

The narrow 15×6-inch wheels and Goodyear G70×15 Polyglas redline tires were for light pedal work only. Anyone serious about winning quickly traded up to larger tires. Standard final drive ratio was 4.10:1, spun through a robust 9.75-inch Dana 60 rear differential to survive the torture dished out by the 440. Either the venerable Chrysler four-speed with a Hurst Competition/Plus shifter or the Pentastar 727 TorqueFlite three-speed automatic brought the power to task. Brakes were four-wheel 11×2.5 manual drums, which were barely adequate at the end of the quarter mile, where trap speeds exceeded 100 miles per hour.

The 1969 Road Runner had an economical base price of $2,945. The A12 became a somewhat popular choice for an additional 15 percent increase of $462.80. A12 Road Runner production lasted only half a year and numbered 1,412 units—615 post models and 797 hardtops. All came adorned with the plain black 15×6 wheels and chrome lug nuts, absent even dog-dish hubcaps.

Color choices for the A12 Road Runner were initially limited to Vitamin C Orange, Performance Red, Bahama Yellow, and a Rallye Green added midyear. Later in production, three additional Dodge colors became available: White, Limelight, and Sunfire Yellow. Interior options were black and white, with a vinyl top also available.

With its lack of normal conveniences, the car was designed to win races. The lift-off fiberglass hood with its giant inlet was lightweight and held on with four racing-style pins. Just checking the oil required two people and a flat surface on which to set the hood.

The first 100 Super Bee A12s were sent to Creative Industries for finishing touches on February 19, 1969, in preparation for the March launch. In all, Chrysler manufactured 3,319 A12s for the 1969½ model year. This performance package was available in both hardtop and two-door post (coupe) bodies but was not offered as a convertible. Only 1,412 of that number were Plymouth Road Runners, with the remaining 1,907 being Super Bees.

When the 440 Six Pack became a standalone option for 1970, it was hidden under the factory hood with only the 440+6 hood callouts to indicate what you were up against. (The feature also became optional on the Charger, Challenger, Coronet, GTX, and 'Cuda.) For 1970 and 1971 the specs changed slightly, including the substitution of a Chrysler cast-iron manifold for the pricier but lighter aluminum Edelbrock intake. The 440+6 option was discontinued at the end of the 1971 model year after 9,271 units had gone out the door in 1970 and an additional 1,158 in 1971. In all, Chrysler produced 13,748 440+6 motors over two and a half years.

➤ While optional bucket seats could be ordered, a good number of the A12 Road Runners came with a full-width front bench seat with vinyl trim.

➤ The heart of the A12 package was the big-block 440 V-8 equipped with three two-barrel Holley carburetors atop an Edelbrock manifold, backed up with a Dana 60 rear axle with 4.10 gears.

↑ Most 1969½ Pontiac GTO Judge package cars included black vinyl interior, although a few escaped with the optional white interior.

THE CAR THAT WAS TO BECOME the 1969 Pontiac GTO Judge was first proposed by Jim Wangers in 1968 as a low-cost Tempest with the GTO 400 motor to counter Plymouth's successful Road Runner. Its midyear launch, like Chrysler's Six-Pack offerings, was designed to sneak under the insurance industry's radar and escape a fat surcharge that might discourage buyers.

Introduced in December 1968 as a mid-1969 model, the concept was to use a Tempest two-door post sedan—the same body design as the popular GTO and the more luxurious LeMans—but equipped specifically for street performance, without luxury appointments. The $332 option featured a 400-cubic-inch Ram Air III producing 366 horsepower, plus dual exhaust and a Posi-Traction limited slip differential. The package also included standard GTO suspension, with Rallye II wheels and G70×14 Goodyear Polyglas tires, but sans the trim ring to save costs. A three-speed T-Handle Hurst shifter was standard, although most purchasers were happy to pay extra for the four-speed manual or even the console-mounted His and Hers Hurst shifter for cars equipped with the automatic option.

When the Judge was released, Pontiac choose to offer the special package in either a two-door hardtop or in a convertible, with the first two thousand units produced in the same vibrant Carousel Red, a shade that was more orange than its name suggested and unavailable on any other Pontiac. The Judge incorporated blacked-out grilles, a urethane front bumper, functional hood scoops, a trunk-mounted wing spoiler, dual sport mirrors, multicolored Judge decals, and side accent stripes. Although a low-cost bench seat was standard, most buyers chose to upgrade to bucket seats. More options meant more profit, though the base price was kept under $3,000 in order to compete directly with the newly released 1968 Plymouth Road Runner.

Buyers could choose the venerable Ram Air IV engine with the Judge package too. Although Pontiac claimed a mere 4-horsepower difference between the III and the IV, at a published 370 horsepower the Ram Air IV was intentionally underrated by approximately 20 horsepower. The number of Judges so equipped has not been documented. We do know that only 700 GTO hardtops and another 59 convertibles were graced with the Ram Air IV hood callouts, with either the four-speed or an automatic driving the power to the pavement. This equates to only 1 percent of the 72,287 GTOs produced for 1969.

Like the Road Runner, the Judge took its name from television. GM executive John DeLorean lifted it from the catchphrase "Here come da Judge," used on the hit program *Rowan & Martin's Laugh-In*. In addition to the popular culture tie-in, the moniker lent itself to ad copy leveraging the rebellious spirit of the time:

1. The Judge can be bought.
2. The Judge. It's justice man, justice.
3. All rise for the Judge.

☚ This first-year Pontiac GTO Judge is well equipped with power front disc brakes, power steering, and Ram Air tub and seal.

⬇ Pontiac chose to keep the Judge package as an addition to the GTO, unlike the Hurst Oldsmobile that shared the base model Cutlass trim and was not a 442.

Pontiac promoted the Judge heavily in print and television ads. Yet ultimately, the package proved more successful in street image than track performance compared to the SC/Rambler or the A12 Road Runner and Super Bee. Looking back, Pontiac's marketing approach of making the car memorable to the average buyer may have been the most successful muscle-car ad strategy.

All in all, the Judge can be considered a sales success, with 6,725 hardtops and 108 convertibles with the Judge package made in 1969 (of 72,287 total 1969 GTOs). It seemed every small town had one Carousel Red Judge holding court on Main Street.

The Judge's sales certainly compared favorably to Chrysler's midyear sales of 3,319 A12s and AMC's 1,512 SC/Ramblers. What all three cars did was raise their respective manufacturers' profiles where it counted: in the showroom. The year 1969 was a good one, when one could acquire a formidable reputation with the purchase of certain new cars. All three offerings were bold in appearance, loud in presence, and memorable in execution.

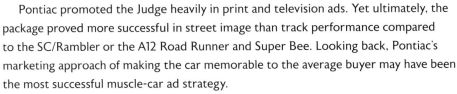

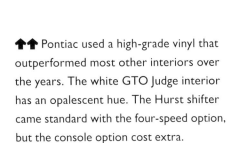

⬆⬆ Pontiac used a high-grade vinyl that outperformed most other interiors over the years. The white GTO Judge interior has an opalescent hue. The Hurst shifter came standard with the four-speed option, but the console option cost extra.

⬆ The interior of the 1969½ Pontiac GTO Judge, with contrasting white bucket seats, is quite sporty looking.

⬆ The 1969 package car "The Judge" in the well-known Carousel Red hue that represented the special GTO midyear model.

⬀⬀ The hood-mounted tachometer was a Pontiac styling trademark in the late 1960s. Although clearly seen here, it was impossible to read at night or in the rain.

➡➡ The GTO Judge received a one-piece rear spoiler that extended over the quarter panels. The owner has added soft foam to the bottom edge to reduce impact when the trunk is slammed.

MANY MUSTANG AND MIDSIZE TORINO OFFERINGS had corresponding models from Ford's sister division, Mercury. Most notable were the Cougar Eliminator models in 1969 and 1970, available with the Trans-Am–inspired Boss 302 engine as well as the 390 and 428 big blocks. Although mentioned in Mercury marketing materials at the time, the Boss 429 single-overhead-cam engine was never produced for street versions of the Cougar. Today the 428-equipped cars get most of the attention, but anyone who has driven the Cougar Eliminator Boss 302 will tell you that the lighter, small-block 302 over the Cougar's front wheels makes for one of the best-balanced pony cars of the era and a formidable sleeper on a winding road.

The Cougar was extensively restyled for 1969, gaining a crisply upmarket, even European exterior that boldly distinguished it from the Mustang. With its subtle front grille treatment, the 1969 edition may be the best-styled Cougar from the classic 1967–1973 era.

Mercury planned to continue with the XR7-G package touting Dan Gurney, captain of Mercury's Sports Car Club of America (SCCA) race team. Gurney had already developed special cylinder heads to help Mercury compete in the Trans-Am series. Ultimately Gurney backed out for 1969, forcing Ford to create a package similar to the Mach 1 or Boss offerings to compete with the Road Runner, Judge, and other fast movers.

The Eliminator name came from the Cougar funny car "Dyno Don" Nicholson campaigned in the NHRA. The name's association with drag racing corresponded with pressure from senior management inside parent Ford Motor Company for Mercury to

➡ All 1969 Cougars had a full grille that was interrupted by a body-color center grille "tooth." The Eliminator package included a horizontal side stripe that ignored the curvaceous body side sculpture.

drop out of the Trans-Am and NASCAR race series, leaving only Ford to compete for manufacturers points toward a season-long championship based on accumulated wins.

The preview for what would become the 1969 Cougar Eliminator first appeared at the Los Angeles Auto Show on October 24, 1968, as part of its Streep Scene exhibit (streep = street + strip). Like the Boss 302, it was designed by GM defector Larry Shinoda.

The show car was finished in arresting Sun Gold pearlescent paint with subtle white graphics. A body-color rear spoiler and American Racing mag wheels further distinguished it from production-version 1969 Cougars. The interior, otherwise pulled from the XR7, featured striking red, orange, and black inserts that would not make the production version introduced the following spring.

A special drivetrain further set the Eliminator concept apart from its progenitors. In back of the 335-horsepower 428 CJ V-8 and robust C6 automatic transmission was a Dana two-speed rear axle. The unit was a modified version the Spicer Model 53 incorporating an overdrive ratio of 0.675:1. Overdrive was engaged via a lever mounted on the console, forward of the storage compartment. Unfortunately the overdrive option did not reach the production Eliminator. Regardless, public reaction at the show was universally positive, after which the Eliminator model was fast-tracked for a midyear introduction. Production began on April 1, 1968, with the first 2,250 Eliminators destined for Hertz for its Sports Car Club program—which the company did not call Rent-A-Racer, despite public use of the term. One hundred and one of these Eliminators took a detour to American Sunroof in Southgate, Michigan, where a sliding-steel sunroof was installed. Records suggest that all of the Hertz Eliminators were equipped with the 351 4V engine and FMX three-speed automatic transmission. Needless to say, a sunroof-equipped 1969 Eliminator is a very rare Cougar.

⬆ The side view of the second-generation 1969 Cougar shows the semifastback design Mercury chose over its assembly line sibling Mustang's full fastback roofline. The Eliminator's addition of the large hood scoop and rear wing add a masculine look to the Cougar line.

↑↑ The 1969 Cougar door panels appeared more luxurious than the previous years plain design with the addition of imitation woodgrain. The full-length console remained an extra-cost option even when the automatic transmission was specified.

↑ The Eliminator package included the 351 four-barrel engine as the standard power plant. A savvy buyer could also choose from the big-block 428 Cobra Jet or the underappreciated Boss 302.

Although the Cougar Eliminator was Mercury's analog to the Mach 1 Mustang, the division's sales could not support two separate performance versions of the Boss Cougar. The Eliminator Boss 302 was simply added as an engine option to the Eliminator package in April 1969, toward the end of the model year. All Boss 302 Cougars were underrated at 290 horsepower and available only through the Eliminator package, which was already rich in upgrades over the standard model.

The Eliminator package was marketed to emphasize performance. While the XR7 was a luxury upgrade over the standard Cougar with only subtle XR7 badges added to the exterior of the car, the Eliminator package was designed to attract and command attention on the street.

In keeping with the focus on speed over comfort, the Eliminator was introduced with a limited choice of colors like the Boss 302. Buyers could choose White, Bright Blue Metallic, Competition Orange, or Bright Yellow. The two FoMoCo performance-package offerings also had stripes and spoilers in common. Due to the Cougar's more formal roofline, it did not include the rear window slat option available for the Mustang. The Eliminator did include a flat-black center hood stripe culminating in a flat black oversized hood scoop that mimicked the Boss 429. Power options ran from the normal 351 4V standard engine to the 428 SCJ Drag Pack. Hidden among the other larger displacement offerings was the Boss 302 engine that was so well suited to the Cougar.

Boss engines paired the 302 block with the high-performance heads from the Cleveland 351 with their larger valves, combined with the high-lift cam and mechanical lifters. They were designed to be high-revving engines. Because air-conditioning compressors were not so freewheeling, both Ford and Mercury excluded this option from the Boss and Super Drag Pack versions of the 428 CJ. The Top-loader four-speed transmission was mandatory for Boss-equipped Cougars.

The cat was 7 inches longer than Ford's equine, with 3 of those inches coming in the Cougar's 110-inch wheelbase. The larger size made the Cougar Eliminator Boss 302 nearly 200 pounds heavier. All things being equal, such as tires and state of tune, the Mustang Boss 302 will be marginally quicker than the Cougar Eliminator Boss 302. Conversely, with its longer wheelbase, weight, and suspension tuning, the Cougar offers a bit more of a comfortable ride.

Introduced late in the 1969 model year, in April 1969, the Boss 302 engine was not advertised or included in the Cougar dealership brochure—one needed to be a Cougar insider to know of the option. As a result, the Boss 302 Eliminator ranks among the rarest series-produced muscle cars. Only 169 Cougars were so equipped in 1969, out of the reported 2,250 built with the Eliminator package.

Because it was offered over more of the 1969 model year, and not technically a midyear model, the 428 CJ Q-Code option found its way under more Cougar hoods in 1969—376 to be exact. (Surprisingly the ram-air R-code was more popular, with 1,164 produced.) Many of the exterior changes, including the blacked-out grille and the large hood scoop, functional with the ram-air option, carried over to the 428-equipped Eliminators. When equipped with the 428 SCJ option, the Cougar Eliminator was a credible straight-line performer: its 0–60 time clocked in at 5.6 seconds, and it covered the quarter mile in 14.1 seconds with a trap speed of 103 miles per hour.

⬆ Continuing with the low and wide theme, the rear taillights were wall-to-wall in appearance, only separated by the need for a hidden gas cap under the center Cougar emblem.

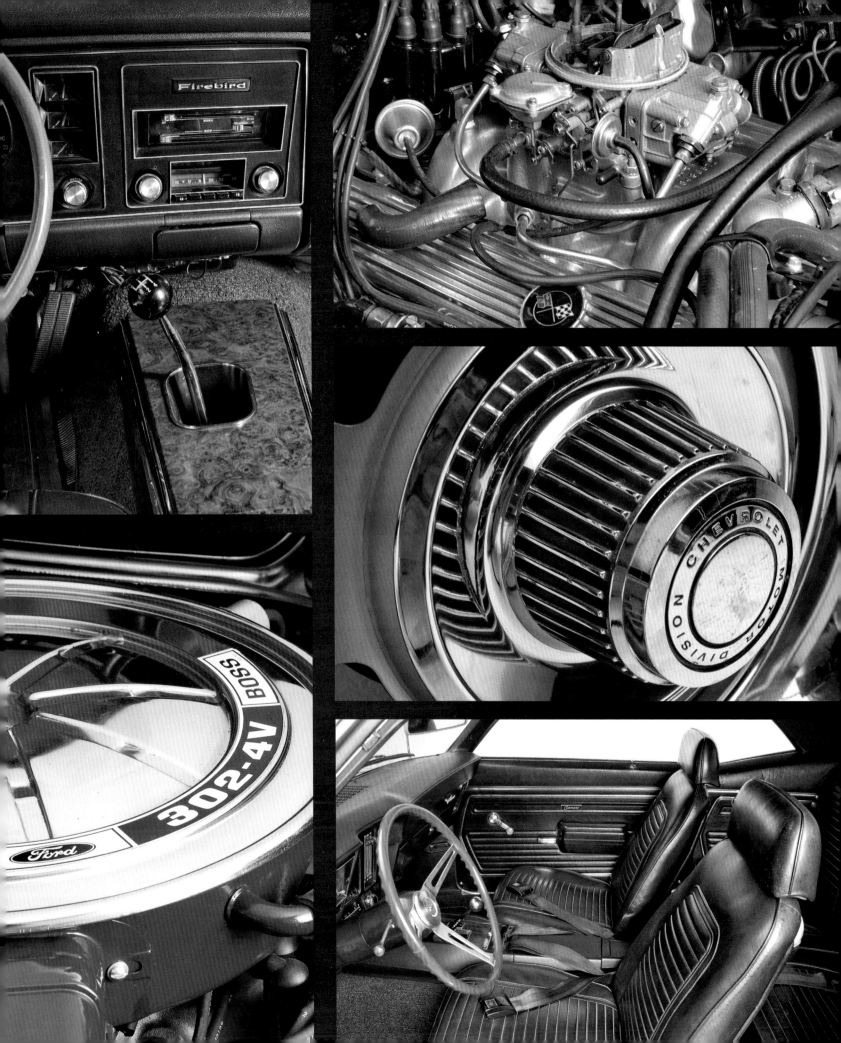

RACE ON SUNDAY . . . .

Trans-Am Cars

Chevrolet Camaro Z/28

Ford Boss 302 Mustang

Pontiac Trans Am

The Trans-Am racing series was created in 1966 for late-model sedans by then president of the Sports Car Club of America, John Bishop. Unlike roundy-round NASCAR and more similar to European Grand Prix races, the Trans-Am series was raced on winding and hilly circuits that required superior handling and braking. Significantly, for the first six years of the series, points were designated to the car manufacturer, not the driver. It wasn't until the 1972 season that drivers received recognition for their season performance.

The series featured two classes based on the cars' engine size: one for those displacing fewer than 2 liters, dominated by foreign cars, and one for engines displacing more than 2 but fewer than 5 liters (305 cubic inches), run by American cars. The series' other major rules were relatively simple: the cars had to have factory-built steel bodies with all glass intact. In most cases, the interior was removed, while the car's suspension, wheels, and tires were enhanced for handling.

In the beginning, the large-displacement division was populated by smaller sedans such as the Dodge Dart and Ford Falcon. When American manufacturers responded to Ford's Mustang with competing models in 1967, however, the Trans-Am series shifted from sedans to pony cars such as the Chevrolet Camaro and Plymouth Barracuda.

⬆ If you were at a stoplight and saw this in your rearview mirror, you knew you were going to be involved in a small-block beat down. The Z/28 version offered fierce acceleration from a standing start.

BY THE SERIES' THIRD YEAR in 1969, the Big Three were eager to promote their performance models by capitalizing on Trans-Am's growing popularity. To achieve that goal, all followed in the footsteps of Chevrolet's successful Z/28 Camaro.

Released as a midyear edition in 1967, the 302-cubic-inch Camaro was designed specifically to compete in the Trans-Am Series. The heart of the car was a new engine based on a 327-cubic-inch block with a forged-steel crank from the legendary 283-cubic-inch small-block. The result displaced just under the series' 305-cubic-inch limit. A dynamic high revver for both the street and the track, it featured solid lifters, larger valves to improve airflow, and a specially designed camshaft that came on over 4,000 rpm and kept pulling to its 7,500-rpm limit. Underrated at 290 horsepower, the 302 produced closer to 350 horsepower, an astounding 1.15 horsepower per cubic inch.

The car was a hidden performer that Chevrolet failed to advertise or even include in any of the factory-produced 1967 brochures. The only way to order it was to start with a base-model Camaro and then add the Regular Production Option (RPO) designated as Z28 (in 1967 there was no hyphen or slash). The option was next in sequence after the Z-27 SS package and similar to the Z-22, which was the RS package. Uprating a base Camaro to Z28 guise cost a whopping $400 in 1967 ($3,200 in 2020 dollars) and yielded the 302 engine, 15-inch Rally wheels, and the F41 handling package. Front-wheel power disc brakes and a four-speed transmission were mandatory. Comfort options such as power steering and air conditioning were unavailable with the Z28 package. Just 602 buyers opted for this configuration in 1967, making it rare today.

When the 1967½ Z28 was released to the public, it had no external Z28 designation other than dual "skunk" stripes on the hood and trunk. In both 1967 and 1968 the engine VIN pad was stamped with *MO* after the last six numbers.

For 1968 the word was out about the Z/28 package (the slash between the Z and 28 was adopted for 1968). Externally the most notable change was a 302 badge on the front fenders. Production increased to 7,199 units, including one Z/28 convertible specially manufactured for a GM executive.

By 1969 the Z/28 Camaro had been out for two years and the performance package was specifically designed to create the foundation of a car that could be easily modified to compete on the track. Two important new options were introduced for 1969. Four-wheel power disc brakes (RPO JL8) were a rare option that only a few buyers chose. This brake option also upgraded the rear springs from the standard monoleaf design to a heavy-duty multileaf to help control wheel hop under hard acceleration. The second upgrade, Corporate Office Production Order (COPO) option 9737, was the Edelbrock dual-carb cross-ram intake manifold. The engine designation changed for 1969, with DZ replacing the previous MO code. By now, the public knew what the Z/28 designation meant and what it could do on the street. A 1969 United Auto Workers (UAW) strike against General Motors delayed introduction of the second-generation 1970 Camaro, resulting in an extended 1969 production year and a total of 20,302 Z/28s for the last year of the first-generation Camaro.

⬆ All factory Z/28 Camaros were shod with 15-inch Rally wheels as compared to the standard Camaro's 14-inch rims.

⬇ The side profile of the Z/28 shows the addition of chrome trim in front of the rear wheels and wheel lip moldings. This detail is often missed on cloned cars.

⬆ The Z/28 had an altered stance compared to other standard Camaros with the edition of four leaf rear springs. Even the side view of the Z/28 includes multiple items with chrome and stainless trim.

➡ All 1969 Z/28 Camaros were factory-equipped with rear bumper guards. The addition of heavy-duty rear springs raised the rear to the point of not meeting the federal bumper height requirements. Chevrolet's fix was to include the rear bumper guards as standard, creating a bumper impact area within the federal guidelines.

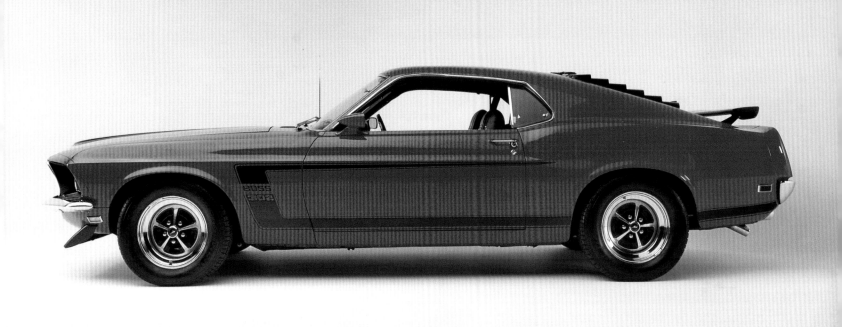

FORD HAD WON the first two seasons of the over-2-liter Trans-Am series. The 1968 field consisted primarily of the larger-displacement Mustangs, Cougars, and Camaros, with the occasional Pontiac Firebird, Dodge Dart, or Plymouth Barracuda. (They raced alongside the lower-displacement series of Alfa Romeo sedans, Porsche 911s, and the occasional Corvair.) For the 1968 showdown of the major pony cars, Mark Donohue dominated the series driving a pair of Z/28 Camaros for the Penske Racing team. The blue and gold Camaros were easy to spot from the stands—attention Ford was determined to regain.

To combat the dominant Camaros, Ford's Boss 302 was essentially a thinly disguised race car for the street. Released on March 27, 1969, the configuration was a $676 option package to the standard Mustang SportsRoof. Reportedly designer Larry Shinoda chose the Boss name in reference to Ford president Bunkie Knudsen, a fellow GM defector who had recruited Shinoda to Ford. The fact that "boss" had a positive slang connotation didn't hurt.

Although the Boss 302 was a late midyear release, Ford had its subcontractor, Kar Kraft, already working to prepare cars in time for the 1969 Trans-Am schedule starting in May. The previous year's three Ford wins paled next to Chevrolet's ten podiums with the Camaro and showed Ford it needed to build a better race car out of the newly restyled 1969 Mustang.

Introduced to the public as a no-frills, race-focused package, it was available in four introductory colors: Calypso Coral (orange), Bright Yellow, Acapulco Blue, and Wimbledon White. It featured a blacked-out grille and tail panel and a front spoiler. The hood and rear deck lid received a similar black-out treatment. The rear wing-style

⬆ The midyear 1969 Mustang Boss 302 was all about balance. The combination of the larger 15-inch chrome Magnum 500 wheels and a factory-lowered stance gave it street cred that was not shared with other factory-built performance cars.

↑ The Boss 302 Mustang was Ford's homologation special built to qualify for the SCCA (Sports Car Club of America) Trans-Am racing series. It carried a base price of $3,669 (about $27,000 in 2021 dollars).

spoiler and rear window slats were extra-cost options, giving the Boss 302 a purposeful look. Dual factory sport mirrors were included, and both sides had a large C-stripe in black reflective tape with *Boss 302* callouts on the front fender sides. Because it was based on the SportsRoof body, it did not have the Mach 1 quarter-panel air scoops.

The heart of the car was its engine. The small-block 302 achieved an impressive 290 horsepower using the new 351 Cleveland wedge-shaped head design with a higher-revving valvetrain that had larger than normal intakes (2.23 inches) and exhausts (1.71 inches). This design combined with larger exhaust ports and free-flowing manifolds to remove the spent gases. The heads had screw-in studs for more strength, with 1.6-ratio rockers controlled by solid lifters and hardened pushrods connecting to a high-lift cam. Ford built on its experience with the legendary 1963–1967 HiPo 289 engine design, only fortified for racing. Using both forged crank and rods and 10.5:1 compression pistons, the small Windsor-built 302 engines were able to create almost 1 horsepower per cubic inch. The 302 block was beefed up with additional webbing and is easily identified by screw-in freeze plugs.

To extend the engine's lifespan, Ford fitted a heavy-duty cooling package and a remote oil cooler. Designers also installed an electronic rev limiter to keep the high-revving engine from flying apart. Unfortunately many owners who battled on the streets discovered the latter feature and bypassed or removed it, leading to engine failure.

An interesting option for the Boss 302 was a four-barrel inline carburetor system atop a specialized two-piece "Cross Boss" intake manifold with a top plenum cover providing space for a single inline four-barrel Autolite 875-cfm carburetor down the center. Although impressive to the eye, this design proved too difficult to manage, and more plenum covers have ended up as garage art than are currently running on cars.

As in drag racing, power-to-weight ratio was critical to performance. The Boss 302 was a hefty 3,417 pounds when equipped as advertised. With 56 percent of that weight at the front and 44 percent at the rear, it was not a perfectly balanced car, especially when most of the components removed for racing were found in the interior and the trunk, increasing front-weight bias in the race-ready version. But Ford was hardly the only builder of the time working with a nose-heavy design.

Standard performance components included quick-ratio steering, a special handling package with front and rear sway bars, and staggered rear shocks. A low ride height to improve cornering required rolled fender lips to avoid interference with the 15×7-inch gray-painted Magnum 500 wheels bearing F60×15 tires. Power front disc and standard rear drum brakes handled haul-down duty. The 9-inch rear end featured standard 3.5:1 gears with an optional locker available. Buyers tuning to drag race could choose 3.91 or 4.30 gearing.

A few final touches rounded out the look. Blackout around the outboard headlights might suggest a hard-brawling streetfighter with black eyes. Crossing another car's path at night, the distinctive Boss 302 reflective stipe down the sides popped when headlights hit it.

The press and the public both viewed the Boss 302 as the little Mustang all grown up. If Ford was looking to shed the conception of the first-generation Mustang being a secretary's car, mission accomplished. The stiff suspension and harsh ride were also not for the average Mustang buyer. Nor was the louder exhaust note counting off each of four gears as the driver notched through them with the factory Hurst shifter.

The first introduction and marketing Boss 302s were pictured with the flat-black hood treatment and no ram-air hood scoop, the idea being that the 1969 Boss 302

⬇ The midyear 1969 Mustang Boss 302 was all about balance. The combination of the larger 15-inch chrome Magnum 500 wheels and a factory-lowered stance gave it street cred that was not shared with other factory-built performance cars.

was a base-model car with limited options and an attractive price. More expensive than the Mach 1, its sales were respectable at 1,628 units, more than twice what Pontiac produced for the first year of its Trans Am (though less than 0.5 percent of the more than three hundred thousand Mustangs produced in 1969).

Kar Kraft prepared the racing Boss 302s from bare bodies in white for the Shelby racing team. Peter Revson, Horst Kwech, Sam Posey, Parnelli Jones, and George Follmer all took their turns piloting the Shelby Boss 302s during the Trans-Am season. Another Boss team formed by Bud Moore also competed in the series. Ford was awarded points toward the championship regardless of which team won.

So how did the Boss 302 pan out on the track? The 1969 season started well with Ford winning four of the first five races, but by July the Penske team's Camaros took over, with Mark Donohue and Ronnie Bucknum shutting out the Ford effort the rest of the way. Not until the following year, when Penske switched to AMC to help develop that automaker's fledgling racing effort, did Follmer and Jones drive the Boss 302 to a championship with six victories in a shortened eleven-race season.

🖤 The flat black tail panel helped identify the 1969 Mustang Boss 302 in traffic as there was no unique model designation visible from the rear. This was the view many drivers saw when a Mustang Boss 302 pulled away from a stoplight.

⬇ The 302-cubic-inch V-8 installed in the Boss 302 Mustangs for 1969 featured cylinder heads redesigned to improve breathing at high RPMs as well as solid lifters.

⬆ The heads on the Boss 302 engines are derived from those found on the Cleveland 351 V-8s.

IF A SINGLE MODEL EPITOMIZED the pony-car presence in the SCCA, it was the one named for the Trans-Am series. That's what you might expect if the vast resources of the big automakers were not constantly barraged and outmaneuvered by shifting views, within and without, that were at least as good at thwarting ambitious goals as advancing them.

Pontiac head John DeLorean wanted a special Firebird to compete with the Z/28 Camaro (let's keep the slash in "Z/28" for simplicity). Pontiac viewed itself as the performance division of GM with a European flair. It had banked heavily on the division-exclusive overhead-cam, six-cylinder engine introduced in the 1967 Firebird and Tempest. Unfortunately consumers weren't wowed. To win those fickle buyers, Pontiac decided to go head-to-head against Chevrolet with a Firebird Trans Am. It licensed the series name from the SCCA for a $5-per-car royalty.

The plan was to develop a 303-cubic-inch engine to squeak under the 5-liter series limit. It would be based on the Pontiac 400-cubic-inch short-decked block but with a new crankshaft and cylinder heads. Research suggests that Pontiac engineering built only four of the engines, none of which was put in a car and released to the public—

⬆ Scoops, stripes, and spoilers all added to the visual effectiveness of the Trans Am package. Although the Polar White was a subtle choice for an image-building muscle car, the Tyrol Blue stripes and body component changes kept the car from being overlooked in traffic.

↑ This side profile view, with no identifying badges, shows the absolute purity in styling of the 1969 Pontiac Firebird Trans Am hardtop.

↗↗ The Trans Am's unique rear taillight panel treatment in Tyrol Blue helped identify the car when following one in traffic. The bold Trans Am spoiler call out was not visible from the street level.

➡➡ With a base price, before options, of $3,556, the 1969 Pontiac Firebird Trans Am was, by design, a rare bird.

so a bit shy of homologation rules' thousand-production-unit minimum for the 2,000 to 5,000cc (305 C.I.) class. DeLorean contracted race-engine designer and retired Australian Formula 1 champion Jack Brabham to develop a 303-cubic-inch, single-over-head-cam, fuel-injected V-8 based on the Pontiac 400-cubic-inch block. Both engine designs proved too expensive for Pontiac's purse.

With engineering creativity stifled, the only thing left for the racing objective was creativity with the rules. Pontiac's TG Racing team was a collaboration between American Jerry Titus and Canadian Terry Godsall. Musing the dilemma of no qualifying Pontiac engine, Godsall realized that Pontiacs manufactured and sold in Canada often used Chevrolet drivetrains. TG Racing submitted paperwork to SCCA showing that the Canadian Firebird was available with the Z/28 302 engine as an option, thus meeting homologation rules. True, no production Firebirds were known to have this option. Nevertheless, TG Racing acquired a 1968 Camaro Z/28 that had been successfully raced by Jon Ward and converted the body to a Firebird. The car finished the last seven races of the 1968 season and gave Pontiac a fourth-place finish behind Chevrolet, Ford, and American Motors. The same car campaigned the 1969 Trans-Am season without changes as a standard 1968 Firebird, bringing the Pontiac team to a third-place finish behind Chevrolet and Ford.

With his vision of conquering Chevrolet for SCCA glory reduced to a single qualifying car—body only—that otherwise was itself a Chevrolet, DeLorean took the practical path. Instead of battling to win a race series called Trans-Am, he would entice the roadgoing public with his Firebird model Trans Am.

The Trans Am performance and appearance package was launched in March 1969, along with the GTO Judge, with surprisingly little fanfare and only one obscure advertisement. The almost $1,200 option was costly on an already expensive pony car. Many were purchased by an older demographic, and sales were less than anticipated, with just 689 Firebird coupes and eight convertibles receiving the Trans Am package. Most of the convertibles may initially have gone to GM executives.

The only alternative to the standard 400-cubic-inch Ram Air III engine rated at 366 horsepower and 435 foot-pounds of torque was the Ram Air IV version with a longer-duration camshaft rated at 370 horsepower and a massive 445 foot-pounds of torque. Ram Air IV engines were ordered on a mere fifty-five Trans Am coupes. (All

Pontiac engines were considered small-blocks even though they would grow to 455 cubic inches.) The standard Trans Am came with a three-speed and 3.55:1 gears, but the Ram Air IV required a four-speed and 3.90:1 cogs. Either version was available with an optional three-speed automatic. The Trans Am package included a heavy-duty suspension with a 1-inch front stabilizer bar, 7-inch-wide rally-style wheels, Goodyear Polyglas F70×l4 whitewalls, and special variable-ratio power steering.

The Trans Am appearance package provided a distinctive-looking Firebird from every angle. All cars were finished in Polar White with Tyrol Blue racing stripes, tail panel, spoiler stanchions, and Trans Am decals. The body had a fiberglass hood with two aggressive hood scoops moved forward, a single functioning engine-compartment air exhaust vent mounted low and aft on each front fender, and a unique 60-inch-wide rear spoiler that touched the top of each quarter panel and required a new heavy-duty trunk spring to keep the lid from slamming shut on the owner.

The standard plush Firebird interior included bucket seats in black, blue, or white with the optional center console included in the Trans Am package. The only Trans Am distinction visible while in the drivers seat is the thin blue twin stripes adorning the hood aimed toward the horizon. The car could be equipped with the optional Firebird gauge package with a tachometer and a 160-mile-per-hour speedometer.

ROUNDY-ROUND:
NASCAR Muscle

Ford Talladega

Mercury Cyclone Spoiler and Spoiler II

Dodge Charger 500

Dodge Charger Daytona

More than fifty million Americans paid to see automobile racing events in 1969. Even President Nixon was amazed by the crowds that were drawn to NASCAR events when he flew over Ontario Motor Speedway on its opening day in his Marine One helicopter and saw more than 125,000 spectators attending. One year later, he would invite 125 racing-industry drivers, crew chiefs, car owners, and automotive parts suppliers to a special White House reception.

Excitement, passion, a sense of movement and freedom were in the air. The previous year, Cale Yarborough had flown a fastback Mercury Cyclone to a 189-mile-per-hour average speed on a qualifying lap with straightaway speeds of 205 miles per hour for the Daytona 500. Even with these spectacular speeds, there remained a heated three-way fight for victory in the NASCAR series.

The 1968 NASCAR season was hotly contested, with Ford, Dodge, and Plymouth racing door handle to door handle at 200 miles per hour. At these speeds, the tiniest excess in wind resistance over a competitor could hold a car from reaching the front. Aerodynamics were critical, and race teams worked with their cars' manufacturers to create slipperier designs.

Ford Talladega

⬆ From the front the aerodynamic design becomes most evident. All Ford Talladegas came in three standard production colors—Presidential Blue, Royal Maroon, and Wimbledon White.

FORD'S ENGINEERS HAD CREATED a great fastback design with a flush rear window, but the Torino front grille was flat and recessed, and it caught the wind like a parachute. Holman-Moody stepped in to help improve the front sheet metal. Using the existing front fender and hood, they designed a smaller grille opening by extending the downward-angled portion of the front hood edge 6 inches with a newly formed filler panel between the front of the hood and the back of the grille opening. To match up with the new top surface, each front fender was cut back 9 inches and a new stamped steel panel about 15.5 inches long hand-welded into place before production.

Holman-Moody's refabrication reduced the car's flat frontal area by about 20 percent. The grille was brought out to the front edge of the extended fenders and sealed with rubber to prevent the wind from swirling in a gap and producing aerodynamic drag. A special brace was fitted to protect the extended, drooped nose from distortion if mechanics leaned on it to check the oil. The front bumper was formed from a flat Torino rear bumper narrowed 18 inches with a V added to the design. It was tucked back to the front edge of the fenders, again to smooth against aerodynamic turmoil where the two components met.

Despite lengthening the car by 6 inches, the Talladega's nose is narrower than the standard Torino's, with less surface area for air to push against. Horsepower spared from fighting wind resistance could now serve its rightful purpose—speed. The hood was painted flat black and retained the chrome *FORD* lettered across the front edge. Because the nose was sealed up and smoothed off, the hood release was activated by a cable run under the dash to a T-handle on the left of the steering column.

Raising the rocker panels 1 inch allowed the race car's front end to be lowered correspondingly without violating NASCAR's ride height requirements. Because more of the inner rocker was exposed with this change, it gave the impression that the inner rocker flange was extended down further than stock. Ford painted the lower rocker black to try to hide the resulting awkward appearance.

The adjustments were worth it, directing air up over the top of the car instead of underneath it. By reducing the Talladega's nose dimensions and driving air over the top of the car, the body changes added 5 miles per hour, or the equivalent of 75 more horsepower.

NASCAR's newest superspeedway (greater than 1 mile around) was built in Talladega, Alabama. Its inaugural event was held in September 1969, and Ford chose to introduce its namesake design at this event. The car was Ford's answer to Dodge's Charger 500, which was also at the race. For 1969 NASCAR rules required that at least 500 of each body design be produced and offered to the public. Ford had already started building the street versions in order to qualify the it for racing.

NASCAR President Bill France Sr. wanted Ford to produce one hundred street cars prior to the race at Daytona. The Holman-Moody team brought him to the Ford warehouse in Atlanta and drove the cars past him as he counted them one by one. As soon as the cars exited the far end of the warehouse the team quietly brought them around to the back of the line. With only three colors produced, the cars all looked the same; by the time France reached the required hundred units, he had counted some of the cars three times.

⬇ The purposeful and understated look of the 1969 Torino Talladega allows it to easily blend into a crowd of normal Ford Torinos, but a sharp eye can detect the specific details that identify the car as a Talladega Special. Notice the lowered rocker moldings below the doors, the extended fenders to reduce drag, and the blacked-out rear taillight panel that were all visual cues of the special package.

→ The 1969 Ford Torino Talladega was powered by the standard 428 Cobra Jet under the hood. No ram air or shaker hoods were used as the car was designed to be aerodynamic. The plan was effective with the Talladega design outperforming the Dodge Daytona and the Plymouth Superbird on NACAR's banked ovals.

Although the design did not involve any major suspension changes, it did use staggered rear shocks that required an unusual sheetmetal box to cover the rough-cut holes in the trunk floor. This box distinguishes a true Talladega, or Mercury's Cyclone Spoiler II, from other Torinos or Montegos.

Compared to some performance packages, the Talladega's exterior details were subtle. Available in only three colors—Presidential Blue, Wimbledon White, and Royal Burgundy—with no wild stripes or outlandish spoilers, the Talladega could easily get lost in a crowd. Only the astute observer noticed the chrome *T* above each door handle, the black-painted tail panel, or the large *T* on the center-mounted gas cap.

Holman-Moody designed the aerodynamic modifications for the car. The manufacturer also created the extended fenders and other pieces used to assemble the 736 documented Talladegas and another estimated 351 Mercury Cyclone Spoiler IIs. There were a total of nine prototype versions as well as five pilot production cars built. Of the prototypes, one became Bunkie Knudsen's daily driver. It was Bright Yellow with a Boss 429 motor and matching color Boss 429 hood scoop. This car started life as a Torino Cobra with white bucket seats and a C6 floor-mounted automatic transmission. It also sported a set of 15×7 chrome Magnum wheels and special side-exiting exhausts when driven by Bunkie. The car survives today and has undergone a full restoration by the Troell family, which has owned it for decades.

◀ The interior of the Ford Talladega Special gives the appearance of a taxicab. No special trim or gauges would help you identify this as anything special. Even when the car is being driven, the sloped front nose disappears without tell-tale muscle car clues such as a hood scoop or special stripes.

▲ The Talladega name was displayed on the interior of the door, providing the driver with the only visual clue to the car's unique provenance.

The rumor that Holman-Moody was contracted to do the final assembly of these cars, like A. O. Smith did for the Shelbys or Kar Kraft did for the Boss 429, is false. All Talladegas and Cyclone Spoiler IIs were built right on the Ford assembly line that produced the standard Torino and Montego. Production reportedly ran from January to February 1969, performed each weekend from early Friday morning through Sunday nights, with Holman-Moody workers helping to assemble the cars at the Atlanta plant.

Each Talladega built was equipped the same way: one of three subdued colors, including the dual sport mirrors painted body color, the bench seat, and the C6 automatic with column shift. Under the flat-black hood was the 335-horsepower "Q-code" 428 CJ with the heavy-duty engine cooling package and a factory oil cooler mounted in front of the radiator support. Normally the oil cooler was available only when the four-speed was specified and when either 3.91 or 4.30 rear gear was added. All street Talladegas received a 3.25 rear-axle ratio.

Inside the cockpit, the Talladega shared the standard Torino black-vinyl interior. The only visible designation was the Talladega decal badge inside each door above the door panel and the T-handled hood release mounted below the dash.

The factory steering wheels were all factory-wrapped with an aftermarket-style, leather-like wheel covers, and all were equipped with an AM radio. The Argent-color GT-style steel wheels bore 14-inch tires with raised white lettering. Other than the AM radio, no other options were included. The package bumped up the cost about $400 over a Torino Cobra for a reasonable sticker price of $3,570.

Mercury Cyclone Spoiler and Spoiler II

MERCURY WAS FIRST INTRODUCED in 1939 as an upscale Ford offering, similar to the relationship between Buick and Chevrolet. As a result, Mercury models tended to be bigger than their Ford counterparts. Thus, as the Cougar was longer and heavier than the Mustang, and the Comet was likewise larger than its Ford analog, the Falcon. For 1969 this difference carried over between the Ford Torino and the Mercury Montego and their NASCAR spin-offs, the Talladega and the Cyclone Spoiler II.

Even though the racing Talladega and Cyclone Spoiler II were a shared concept in NASCAR, the engines offered to the public differed. For production versions of the Mercury, the 351 4V 290-horsepower V-8 was standard. The ram-air R-code 335-horsepower 428 CJ was optional. Records indicate that only fifty-seven production units were equipped with this option. All of these would have the traditional short Montego "W" nose, named for the suggestion of the letter's shape from a bird's-eye view of the car's front end—the contours of the leading front fender edges, inset grille, and protruding center portion of the hood form a wide, shallow W.

Mercury offered Cale Yarborough and Dan Gurney special versions of the Cyclone Spoiler and Cyclone Spoiler II. Each car was primarily Wimbledon White with red and blue accents. Those cars designated as Cale Yarborough Specials were painted with a Candy Apple Red roof, red side hockey stripe, and had matching red interior. The Dan Gurney version had a Presidential Blue roof, blue side hockey stripes, and matching blue interior. All Cyclone Spoilers were equipped with an adjustable wing rear spoiler painted to match the roof. Additionally, the body shape offered on the Cyclone Spoiler retained the normal Montego (W) front end, and the Cyclone Spoiler II shared the drop-snoot aero design similar to the Torino Talladega's.

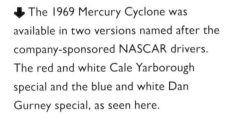

⬇ The 1969 Mercury Cyclone was available in two versions named after the company-sponsored NASCAR drivers. The red and white Cale Yarborough special and the blue and white Dan Gurney special, as seen here.

The Spoiler II's nose is longer and has a slightly steeper angle due to the front lip of the stock hood. This 35-degree angle versus the Talladega's shallower 30-degree angle allowed the racing Spoiler II to achieve a top speed up to 5 miles per hour faster than the track Talladega. Although both the Talladega and Spoiler II appear to have identical bodies, they only shared a few common components in the doors, trunk lids, updated bumper, and grille. The Mercury Cyclone Spoiler II won eight Grand National races (now the Monster Cup) during the 1969 and 1970 NASCAR seasons.

Mercury released the public cars with virtually no fanfare or marketing support. The actual number of Mercury Cyclone Spoilers versus Spoiler IIs is uncertain. When they were gathered to be counted for homologation purposes, Mercury strategically placed the aero-nose versions closest to the inspection point and along the outside edges, filling the middle with the 152 Cyclone Spoilers with their standard front sheet-metal design. Since they were all painted with the distinctive blue and red roofs, they were easy to count from a distance.

The total official NASCAR count was 503 units produced, and the cars were homologated for racing. This suggests that 351 Cyclone Spoiler IIs formed the balance of the 503, but Mercury records have not been found to verify these totals. The Cyclone Spoiler cars, which did not receive the aero-nose design, were also not limited to the option choices the Spoiler II cars had. For this reason it is common to find bucket seats, the 390 engine, and even four-speed cars in the W-nose Cyclone Spoiler version.

↑ The 1969 Mercury Cyclone came with the standard W-shaped nose or this more sought after aero-nose version that shared its origins with the Talladega Ford. The white with blue trim designates this as a Dan Gurney special edition.

Boss 429 Mustang: Hi-Po Pony

FORD INTRODUCED THE PUBLIC to both the Boss 302 and the Boss 429 in January 1969. The Boss 302 was slated as a Z/28 Camaro competitor for both the street and the track. The Boss 429 did not really have a direct competitor in either setting. Other than the big-block Mustang and the Cougar with the 428 CJ, there wasn't an existing pony car with an engine over 400 cubic inches that was eating up a road course. Most pony cars meant for curvy tracks were designed with high-revving small-blocks, which allowed better handling and less weight to slow down with braking.

The Boss 429's only real design purpose could have been as a monster-engined pony car to compete at drag races, but two problems kept it from dominating the quarter-mile: One, because the Boss engine was unique, with a cast block and special aluminum heads, there was a lack of aftermarket support for performance parts. Two, because the Boss 429 came with only four-speed transmission, Ford was required to have the thermactor pollution control with an air pump and stock-style exhaust manifolds on each car produced. The Boss 429 received a 735-cfm Holley carb while the Boss 302 received a 780-cfm one. One can only conclude that the Boss 429 needed to be tamed with a bit of fuel and air deprivation as well as a rev limiter to keep the NASCAR-designed motor together long enough for the consumer's warranty to expire.

The Boss 429 package began as a standard Mustang SportsRoof body, to which the Rouge factory assembly line applied newly designed shock towers, rolled front fenders, and a three-quarter rear sway bar and moved the battery tray to the trunk. The finished and painted body then went to Kar Kraft, which shoehorned the Boss 429 motor into the engine bay. With subtle colors and minimal external fanfare other than the massive hood scoop, the new brute was first known to many as a set of taillights fading in the distance.

The first year there were two different versions of the Boss 429 motor. The earliest 1969 Boss 429s received the S-code engines; these had hefty connecting rods with ½-inch rod bolts, whereas the later T-code engines used lighter, strengthened rods. The theory on the switch is that the first 279 cars received the NASCAR rods, while the rest got lighter rods that allowed the engine to rev quicker. Both engines were sold short of their true potential, but few customers wanted to pay the exorbitant price to own a Boss 429 only to violate the warranty by reworking the engine to realize its peak performance.

Additionally this expensive pony car was short on comfort. No air-conditioning, power steering, or cruising-oriented rear gears were available. You had to be a serious motorhead to walk into your local Ford dealer and choose the "Boss Nine" for commuting to work in any type of freeway traffic. However, Ford was able to sell enough to meet the NASCAR engine requirement, with 859 units made. Many Boss 429s were driven sparingly and have survived as unaltered collector cars with extremely low miles. Creating this number of 1969 Boss 429 Mustangs for public consumption also made the 429-engined Talladega and Cyclone Spoiler II eligible to race in NASCAR-sanctioned events. Mustang Boss 429 production was not sufficient to satisfy the homologation requirements until the Atlanta Race on March 30, 1969, when the Boss engine could officially race.

The combination of the aero body and Boss engine worked so well that Ford kept the recipe in place for the next three years. Contrary to popular belief, Ford won the aero wars in the first round. Not only did the automaker bring the king of NASCAR, Richard Petty, to the Blue Oval in 1969, but it would go on to win twenty-nine Grand National races that year. Even though it lost Richard Petty back to Plymouth when it introduced the 1970 Superbird, 1969 was a spectacular year for Ford and its championship-winning driver, David Pearson.

➔➔ The 1969 Ford Mustang Boss 429 cost a staggering $3,826. It was that year's most expensive Mustang and most carried a bottom-line sticker of close to $5,000.
➔➔ The Boss 429 engine, which produced 375 horsepower, fills up this 1969 Ford Mustang's engine compartment.

DODGE INTRODUCED THE AERO-NOSE Charger 500, complete with flush-mounted rear glass to replace the recessed rear window, in October 1968. Richard Petty had asked for a Plymouth version of the Dodge 500 to compete against the Torino design first introduced in the 1968 season. When Plymouth told Petty no, he packed his bags and went over to Ford to remain competitive.

Ford upped its aero game with the Talladega and Cyclone Spoiler II, produced in January 1969 and first raced in February 1969. Dodge's next salvo would be released in the spring of 1969 and first raced in September 1969: the wildly designed Dodge Daytona with both a pointed nose and an oversized rear wing. By then Plymouth saw the need to play along and create its own version, which was enough to bring King Richard back to his prior domain.

All these aero cars with their 7-liter motors were capable of crossing the 200-mile-per-hour threshold on the longer superspeedways. However, the downforce allowing them to push to such speeds was destroying the tires keeping the cars on the track. So great were the dangers that the front-running drivers withdrew from the late season 1969 Talladega race due to a rash of dangerous tire failures, mainly by Firestone. Goodyear had introduced a new high-speed tire at this race that could survive the Daytona's straightaway speeds throughout the race, giving Richard Brickhouse a chance to place his name in the history book. (Ironically, neither the Dodge Daytona nor the Ford Talladega won at its namesake track in 1969—instead, each won at the other's.)

Although all public versions of the Talladega received the Q-code 428 engine, the NASCAR track versions never used that motor. The first aero-bodied cars were raced with the 427-cubic-inch tunnel-port design, but Bill France brought up the fact that the public could not purchase a new Ford with that engine. Ford's response was unique in that it chose to homologate the 429 engine separately from the body it would be raced in. No other manufacturer would attempt or achieve this move.

⬆⬆ The Charger 500 grille and headlights are moved forward to eliminate any air becoming trapped in the standard grille cavity.

⬆ Although the rear taillights are standard 1969 fare, an attentive observer will identify the flush rear window as one of the special midyear 1969 Charger 500s.

➡ The use of the Coronet grille gives the Charger body an odd family resemblance. From this angle the Charger almost looks pedestrian with few signs that a monstrous Hemi resides under the unadorned hood.

⬆ The Dodge Charger 500 appears bloated around the rear C-pillars with its curved rear window. Although this improved airflow over the car's skin, it still did not achieve the high speeds sought after on the NASCAR circuit.

⬅ Body-painted wheels with dog-dish hubcaps and a subtle gold color hide the high-speed capabilities of this midyear production car.

Dodge Charger Daytona

↥ The rounded rear window replaced the deeply recessed rear window found on the non-Daytona Chargers. This change created a dramatic reduction in drag and helped the aerodynamics of the car.

IT WAS APPARENT THAT the Dodge Charger 500, with its flush front grille and redesigned flush rear backlight (rear window), was a stopgap measure. With no Plymouth version in the works, Richard Petty transferred the Petty Blue #43 livery to the Ford Torino Talladega. Even with the 500's aerodynamic improvements over the stock Dodge Charger, it still wasn't competitive with the Torino Talladega and Mercury Cyclone Spoiler at speed on the high banks.

It soon became obvious that if Dodge wanted to win in NASCAR, they would need to create a more radical aerodynamic approach. Chrysler had a rocket production division based in Huntsville, Alabama, which was the primary contractor for the first stage of the Saturn V booster that would take Neil Armstrong and Buzz Aldrin to the surface of the Moon in July 1969. From the Huntsville missile group, Chrysler plucked an actual rocket scientist, John Pointer, to improve the aerodynamics of the Charger 500. Pointer and the team's leader, Larry Rathgeb, along with a dedicated group at Chrysler's Highland Park, Michigan, headquarters, developed what was to become the 1969 Dodge Charger Daytona. It was one of the first instances in which wind tunnel testing helped develop a production car (if making the NASCAR-required 500 units was considered a production car).

The first prototype was taken to Chrysler's top-secret Chelsea Proving Grounds, west of Detroit, for testing. There, on Chrysler's high-banked oval, it lapped the course at more than 204 miles per hour. It was at a time when Detroit's automakers used spy aircraft to keep tabs on each other's developments, and Ford reportedly had eyes in the sky keeping tabs on the goings-on during the Daytona's high-speed runs.

Dodge knew that NASCAR would put the radical new Charger Daytona under intense scrutiny, requiring proof of the requisite 500 production units before allowing it to race. With the car set to debut at the late-summer Talladega 500 in Alabama, Chrysler awarded the post-production contract to Creative Industries to meet the required production.

Detroit OEMs regarded Creative Industries as a company to whom they could entrust important (and secret) programs. There was a big problem, however: the track at the brand-new Talladega Motor Speedway was paved with a compound that destroyed tires, making the track unsafe in the eyes of many drivers. This led to the attempted formation of a driver's union headed up by none other than Richard Petty. Most of the best-known NASCAR drivers boycotted the race, with Richard Brickhouse, in the #99 Dodge Charger Daytona, scoring his one and only series win.

Back in Michigan, Creative Industries completed a reported run of 503 cars. (Some sources indicate that five additional cars were produced for Canadian customers.)

The standard engine for the production cars was Dodge's four-barrel version of its 440 V-8, rated for 375 horsepower at 4,600 rpm. The base price came in at a whopping $3,993 (about $30,000 in 2021 dollars—less than half the price of a 2021 Dodge Charger Hellcat). Of course, like other Chrysler B-bodies that year, there were two

⬆ This shot showcases the definitive element of the 1969 Dodge Charger Daytona: its 18-inch nose cone that—combined with the rear wing—provided maximum downforce for NASCAR's superspeedways.

⬇ At Talladega in the summer of 1969, Dodge debuted the Charger Daytona, which took the aero-specific modifications of the previous Charger 500 to the next level by replacing the flush grille with an 18-inch nose cone after the Charger 500's inability to compete on NASCAR's superspeedways.

The snap-on fuel filler door and the rear-mounted wing combine to mark the rear quarter of the Dodge Charger as one of the most distinctive muscle cars of all time.

With its distinctive dual snorkel air cleaner, this is the version of the 440-cubic-inch V-8 offered not only in the 1969 Dodge Charger but other Mopar B-body muscle cars. It produced 370 horsepower at 4,600 rpm.

higher-powered options available in 1969. First up was the 440-cubic-inch Six-Pack option featuring three two-barrel carbs atop an Edelbrock intake and producing a reported 390 horsepower as a dealer-installed option.

The top factory-installed engine option, found only on seventy documented cars, was the all-powerful 426 Hemi. It produced an underrated 425 advertised horsepower and added $648.20 to the bottom line on the sticker.

Each of the 503 cars built featured the unique 18-inch nose cone with pop-up headlights, as well as the Charger 500's flush-mounted rear backlight (rear window) and a 23-inch-tall adjustable wing on the rear deck. Each car subassembled at the Creative Industries facility included modified front fenders that would be used on the upcoming 1970 Chargers with the addition of the fender-top cooling scoops and a lengthened hood assembly. All modifications contributed to the car's state-of-the-art 0.28 coefficient of drag (Cd), which was an extraordinary achievement for the time.

While the 1969 Charger Daytonas, with their late-season appearance, did turn the tide for Dodge to a degree, it was simply not enough to outpace the Fords. David Pearson, driving an aerodynamic Ford Torino Talladega, won eleven races en route to claiming the 1969 Grand National Championship, his third of three championships. Richard Petty, with ten wins for the season, placed second to Pearson. Bobby Isaac, in a Charger Daytona, finished in sixth place, with seventeen wins, most on the Grand National circuit that year. In summer 1969, just before the 1970 models arrived at dealers, the 1969 Dodge Charger Daytonas rolled off transporters at dealers from coast to coast.

With just 503 cars built, not every dealer received one. (This was an issue that NASCAR would attempt to address in 1970 with the Plymouth Road Runner Superbird program that lured Richard Petty back to the Mopar fold, stipulating that one Superbird be built for every two Plymouth dealers.)

For their December issue, *Road Test* magazine finally got a chance to road-test the 1969 Charger Daytona (there would be no 1970 version). Equipped with the 440 four-barrel, it covered the quarter mile in 14.48 seconds with a trap speed of 96.15 mph. That same month, *Car and Driver* tested the 426 version, reporting it covered the quarter mile in 13.9 seconds at 101 mph.

The racing life of the 1969 Dodge Charger Daytona (and that of the Plymouth Road Runner Superbird) would be short. In 1971, to get speeds under control, NASCAR limited engine displacement for the low-production aero cars to just 305-cubic-inches, rendering the cars virtually uncompetitive. Soon the big wings would be a NASCAR memory.

For years after, several of the civilian versions of the so-called "Winged Warriors" reportedly languished on dealer lots, some into 1973 when the first OPEC oil embargo hit. Though unconfirmed, it is said that some dealers in desperation removed the aero components and sold the cars (especially the Superbirds) as production Chargers and Road Runners. If true, this stands in stark contrast to these cars' desirable standing among collectors today. Because of their rarity, they are the holy grail of Mopar performance—especially the Hemi-powered cars.

It's interesting to note, forty-five years later, that a box stock, thick-as-a-brick 2020 Dodge Charger Hellcat, the spiritual successor to the 1969 Dodge Charger Daytona, has a documented top speed of 204 miles per hour. It goes to show just how far our production cars have come.

In 2020 two of the individuals who were instrumental in the development of the 1969 Dodge Charger Daytona and 1970 Plymouth Road Runner Superbird turned their last laps. Gary Romberg passed away on January 15, 2020, age eighty-five. Two months later, his one-time colleague, Larry Rathgeb, died of COVID-19-related complications on March 22, 2020. Both were responsible for the success and the legacy of Chrysler's bold two-year program to dominate NASCAR's high-banked ovals, and both left a permanent reminder of their design capabilities. May they both race in peace.

⬆ The 1969 Dodge Charger Daytona and the 1970 Plymouth Road Runner Superbird may have a similar appearance due to the sloped nose and large rear spoiler, but none of the body components are interchangeable.

While most 1969½ muscle-car "package" models were built and released specifically to meet homologation requirements for the different race series, the 1970 offerings were designed and marketed to a different concept—that true muscle cost true money.

During the late 1960s General Motors had lived under a self-imposed cap on the cubic inches it would allow in the midsize A- and F-bodied muscle cars. The Chevrolet Chevelle/Malibu, Buick Skylark/GS, Pontiac LeMans/GTO, Oldsmobile Cutlass/442, and Camaro and Firebird twins all had a corporate limit of 400 cubic inches. This rule was formally abandoned for 1970 after being systematically ignored during the 1969 model year.

Right under the noses of the pinstripe suits, GM divisions had broken the rules with a performance production system that obscured who was suppling what and where. The workaround recipe was developed through relationships like Hurst's with Oldsmobile and later with Chevrolet and dealers like Dana, Berger, Gibb, and Yenko.

Hurst had proposed a Toronado 455–powered midsize Cutlass for 1968, but the idea ran afoul of the corporate restrictions. Applying mechanical aptitude to the corporate machine, George Hurst and Oldsmobile devised a plan for a special order

of Peruvian Silver Cutlasses in which Hurst would replace the factory 400-cubic-inch powerplant with the massive 455 among other work at its facility in Lansing, Michigan. The cars would then be returned to Oldsmobile's distribution network to be shipped to participating dealers and sold as a special collaboration Hurst/Olds.

Parsing the process and costs, the players concluded that it would be more economical if Hurst weren't tasked with removing and replacing engines during the conversion process. Thus, unbeknownst to senior management, all of the 1968 and 1969 Hurst/Olds manufactured were produced with the 455 Oldsmobile engine installed at the factory. To maintain the spirit, if not the practice, of the displacement rule, the paperwork showed that the engines were purchased separately—but all of them were installed by Oldsmobile, not Hurst, flagrantly breaking the General Motors edict.

Similar sleight of hand allowed a few Chevrolet performance dealers to sell 427 Camaros, Chevelles, and Novas in 1968. Motion Performance in New York, Yenko Chevrolet in Pennsylvania, Dana Chevrolet in California were all creating their version of the ultimate muscle car. Fred Gibb of Gibb Chevrolet was a pioneer in the quest for the factory-built muscle car. Gibb felt that the big-block 396 cubic-inch,

➡ The Chevelle dash was finished in low glare, matte black finish with deeply recessed gauges. The tachometer was redlined at 6,500 rpm for the LS6 450-horsepower 454.

375-horsepower 1968 Chevy II Nova could be a heavy hitter in the NHRA's automatic transmission class—if the transmission were available for the car. He found a path for his goal by ordering fifty 1968 L78 Novas fitted with M40 Turbo Hydra-matics using the Corporate Office Production Order (COPO) system. The COPO order program was normally used for fleet applications and Fred Gibbs' order did not violate the 400-cubic-inch ceiling that GM corporate had imposed. In the following model year, this creative order process would allow other Chevrolet performance dealers to tap the COPO conduit in order to build specialty muscle cars skirting the 400-cubic-inch capacity limit for certain model lines.

In 1969 Chevrolet product manager Vince Piggins devised a plan that would create a COPO specifically to put the L72 Corvette 427-cubic-inch, 425-horsepower motor in Camaro and Chevelle bodies. Normally reserved for fleet purchases requiring special equipment or a municipality's specific paint color, the COPO program was now used to create a fleet-purchase super muscle car. The COPO package #9561 went beyond the massive L72 motor and included the F41 heavy-duty suspension with either the M20 or M21 four-speed transmission or the Turbo Hydramatic 400 three-speed automatic transmission with a rear-end ratio of 4.10:1.

Number 9561 included RPO L72, a 427-cubic-inch four-bolt main cast-iron block with 11.0:1 compression-forged aluminum pistons, forged steel rods, and a forged steel crank. The factory camshaft measured 302/316-degree solid with a hefty 0.520 lift. The engine breathed through large 2.19-inch intake and 1.71-inch exhaust steel alloy valves. A Holley 780-cfm four-barrel carburetor attached to the aluminum intake manifold. Special chambered exhaust helped the big-block breath and added the characteristic street-legal sound to the package. The result was an impressive 425 horsepower at 5,600 rpm and 460 foot-pounds of torque at 4,000 rpm.

With the additional cubic inches came additional weight over the front wheels. The COPO cars required power front disc brakes, heavy-duty four-core radiators, and heavy-duty twelve-bolt rear axles.

An additional COPO program, #9560, provided the aluminum-block and aluminum-head 427-cubic-inch ZL1 which included the new transistorized ignition for an additional $4,160 over the base price of the Camaro. Because they came through the established COPO program, the cast-iron and all-aluminum 427 V-8s were not exempt from warranties and were totally street legal.

◀ The 1970 Rebel Machine's Hurst shifter retained the factory round ball and not the more hip, formed T-handle.

➡ The engine compartment of the 1968–1970 B-body Mopars was designed from the start to accommodate the 440 big-block V-8s.

Customers ordered the L72 COPO #9561 on 1,015 Camaros along with an additional 69 of the Aluminum ZL1 under #9560. Most of the public was unaware that these cars roamed the streets and fought on the drag strips. The former packages eliminated the traditional engine displacement numbers from the outside of the car. One of the only giveaways was the mandatory ZL2 cowl induction hood and the absence of any external factory striping. Most COPOs were ordered with body-color plain 14×7 steel wheels with dog-dish caps. The Super Sport (SS) package was not available as an option to the COPO cars, but the hidden-headlight Rallye Sport (RS) option was, and it was found on 193 of the 427 Camaros. Other common Camaro options included vinyl top or front and rear spoilers.

Yenko Chevrolet started the program by ordering 201 of these COPOs, with Berger Chevrolet committing to another 50 units. Other Chevrolet performance dealers made up the balance of the production run of a little over 1,000 units.

An additional 200 Chevelle L72 427 COPO cars were built in 1969 with the majority going through the capable hands of Yenko Chevrolet. Both the Camaros and the Chevelles sold by Yenko included special *YSC* (Yenko Super Car) stenciling on the headrests as well as a unique full-length side decal stripe with *Yenko SC* high on each rear quarter panel denoting the special edition.

General Motors removed the cubic-inch limit for the 1970 model year. In order to be ready for production with the new larger 454-cubic-inch engines, the engineering department must have known at least a year in advance that the restraints were about to be lifted. Whether the expanded COPO program had been a test of this process or just the changing market conditions, all four divisions had a running start at 1970 with over-400-cubic-inch displacements.

With the diversity of direction that GM chose to show for 1970 came an equally diverse change in marketing. The package cars released midyear 1969 were all conscious of both the up-front cost to the consumer and the insurance premiums incurred by performance models. For 1970 the marketing approach was more toward the well-heeled muscle-car buyer. Gone were the taxicab vinyl interiors in drab gray, and no longer would you need to have biceps like George Foreman in order to park your muscle car. Power steering, automatic transmissions, and even factory air-conditioning to keep you from sweating while waiting your turn in traffic were now available at a cost.

More power translated to more money for 1970, with buyers ticking off option boxes they had ignored or been deprived of in previous years. It was not uncommon to see new muscle cars approaching a $5,000 sticker price, whereas sticker prices around $3,000 for the midyear 1969 introductions were commonplace just six months earlier.

The marketing departments took this to heart as well, pitching to a broad audience interested in fully optioned cars. Some of the special editions from midyear 1969 continued into

← For 1970, Ford found homes for 499 Boss 429 Mustangs. With a base price of $3,826, Ford likely lost money on every Boss 429 Mustang it sold to the general public.

the 1970 model year under these considerations—cars such as the Judge, Trans Am, Boss 302 and 429, and Cougar Eliminator and Cyclone—while others stingily targeted at speed and homologation, such as the SC/Rambler, Talladega, and Daytona, disappeared, having served their purpose.

Even with the additional marketing and profitability of the higher optioned cars for 1970, the cards were stacked against average buyers getting the car of their dreams. The UAW strike in 1970 affected almost 350,000 GM workers in the United States and Canada. With the strike consuming more than two months at the beginning of the production year, most GM dealers had no stock of the current year's muscle car offerings. For this reason, many of the 1970 GM cars were special ordered by their first buyers, who could not buy off the lot, while other GM customers switched brands rather than wait.

The strike accomplished a 30 percent wage increase over three years, resulting in an average of 50 cents more per hour for each worker for the first year, increasing to an additional $1.80 per hour over three years. The other car manufacturers followed suit with similar increases for their workers.

Another unusual event affected GM's F-body second-generation Chevrolet Camaro and Pontiac Firebird. Production for this new design was expected to begin in August 1969 but actually didn't began until February 1970. The delay was due to manufacturing complications with the large rear quarter panels. At the final die tryouts before production was to

begin, the Fisher Body facilities discovered that the new quarter-panel design was prone to wrinkling and splitting. GM chose to reconfigure the draw dies that were used to stamp out the rear panels from flat sheet stock. The company expected a short delay, but the resulting changes did not solve the problem. The issue forced GM to revise the process, instead using two sets of dies to form the panels in two steps. Implementing the new setup kept the Camaro and Firebird out of buyers' hands until February 1970.

While the sky was the limit for horsepower ratings in 1970, the end of an era was peeking around the corner. Domestic manufacturers had been banking on the muscle-car market to help bolster sales for this year, only to find total sales figures flat or slightly lower than the prior year. The only manufacturer that saw an increase over its previous year's production was Ford, which saw a 10 percent increase to once again top the two-million-unit mark after three years slightly below that threshold.

Other manufacturers were spared from the impact of the strike with the exception of American Motors, which saw a 10 percent drop in sales due to the thirty-day strike at its facility in Kenosha, Wisconsin. The expectation for Chevrolet had been that 1970 would be the peak of performance and sales. Instead, it built six hundred thousand fewer cars. Few true muscle cars survived into the 1971 model year, and by 1972, the muscle car made but a soft echo of its loud entrance into the new decade.

Chevrolet

Whenever people discuss the ultimate muscle car, talk quickly turns to the ultimate powerplant of the era. All three contenders for ultimate engine were available new for only two years: Ford's Boss 429 was available for half of 1969 through 1970. Chevrolet's LS6 engine could be had in 1970 with a few creeping into the 1971 production year. The Chrysler Hemi was introduced in the larger cars in the mid-1960s and finally offered in the new E-body for 1970 and 1971.

The overlap of all three of these behemoth air pumps was for one model year, 1970. Yet the debate over which made the ultimate muscle car has more to do with memories than statistics. Each fan who was alive when this machinery was introduced and during the subsequent years when it made for rolling, roaring art in Hometown USA has a memory and a formidable firsthand story of their youthful lust over one or more of these champions.

Big-Block Chevelle L34/LS6

Camaro Z/28

Camaro SS 396 L78

Nova SS 396 L78/L89

Big-Block Chevelle L34/LS6

↑ Top down or top up, a big-block Chevelle SS with either the 396 or 454 engine was one of the most feared ragtops of its era.

IN 1969 a special COPO order had been required to purchase the largest-displacement 427 Chevrolet motor in the subframe of the Camaro or the full frame of the Chevelle SS. Chevrolet's big-block had first appeared in a midsize body as a 375-horsepower, 396-cubic-inch mechanical lifter motor in the 1965 Z/16 Chevelle SS. This same basic design had now grown to 454 cubic inches and was rated at 450 ground-pounding horses. No other carbureted mass-production car would ever come from Detroit with a higher horsepower rating.

The basic Chevelle SS hardtop (Z25) included the L34 396-cubic-inch engine and was priced at $3,497, with a convertible option available for an additional $200. The Super Sport package was also available in the car-based pick up, the El Camino SS. The new-car buyer in 1970 had a choice to upgrade the SS package with one of two optional 454 engine configurations: the baseline 454 engine, designated LS5, or the Hemi-beating LS6, rated at just under 1 horsepower per cubic inch.

Because its options list was longer, a fully equipped LS5 SS could have a higher sticker price than an LS6 Chevelle SS even though the latter had more horses. Of the 53,599 Chevelle SS and El Camino SS units made that year, only 8,733 buyers opted for the SS454 package. A little over half of the 8,773 SS454 buyers were savvy enough to purchase the LS6 option—4,475 units reported, or 8 percent of SS production.

In comparison, Chrysler's total 426 Hemi production over eight years, from 1964 to 1971, tallied 6,671 cars as reported by Chrysler. Chevrolet's LS6 was produced for just two years with a total of 4,663 units, or 70 percent of the total 426 Hemi production.

Total Malibu/Chevelle SS/El Camino production for 1970 was 489,582 units, of which 435,970 units were non–Super Sport models. Of the 53,612 SS produced in this year, the engine breakdown was as follows:

- L34 was the 396-cubic-inch rated at 350 horsepower, with 44,826 units made (84 percent of SS Chevelle production).
- L78 396/375 horsepower was available early in the year, with only thirteen reported built. L89 aluminum heads were available for this motor as an option.
- LS5 454 was rated at 360 horsepower at 5,600 rpm and 500 foot-pounds of torque using a hydraulic camshaft and cast-iron intake, Rochester carburetor, and 11.25:1 compression. The 4,298 made constituted about 9 percent of SS production.
- LS6 454 was rated at 450 horsepower at 5,600 rpm with 500 foot-pounds of torque with a solid lifter cam, aluminum intake, Holley 800-cfm carb, 11.25:1 compression ratio, and 6,250-rpm redline, with most performance shifts happening north of 5,000 revs. This option accounted for 4,475 units, or about 10 percent of Chevelle SSs made in 1970.
- LS7 was rated at 465 horsepower at 5,600 rpm with 500 foot-pounds of torque with a high-performance solid lifter cam, aluminum intake, and Holley carb. It's estimated that fewer than two hundred over-the-counter engines were made.

The motor was the heart of the big-block Chevelle Super Sport. Based on the lower-cost Malibu midsize model, the Super Sport package changed the name to Chevelle SS and was available only in the two-door hardtop and the convertible body styles.

Both the 1970 Malibu and Chevelle SS were revised versions of the 1968–1969 body design, with the quad headlights and body-color headlight surrounds similar to the urethane front bumper design on the GTO. The taillights had been removed from the rear-end caps and integrated into the rear bumper, with single rectangular taillights set outside of the rubber bumper overlay clearly marked with an embossed *SS* designation.

All LS6 Chevelle SSs came with the ZL2 functional cowl hood and the dual wide longitudinal stripes on the hood and trunk. These stripes could be factory deleted if so specified.

⬇ While some might prefer rowing the gears of a Muncie heavy-duty four-speed manual, this SS454 is equipped with a Turbo Hydramatic 400 three-speed automatic transmission.

⬇⬇ In 1970, Chevrolet offered what can be considered the ultimate muscle car convertible, the Chevelle available with either a 396- or 454-cubic-inch V-8. This is an SS 396, which was rated at 350 horsepower.

➡➡ 1970 Chevelle Super Sport can be identified by the "SS" rubber bumper overlay and the one-year-only rectangular taillights. The 1971 SS carried over the same distinguishable body style but had four round taillights integrated into the rear bumper.

🢓🢓 For 1970 the Chevelle displayed a large SS emblem in the center of the blacked-out grille. Not all SS Chevelles received the oversize skunk stripes. Savvy street racers learned to read the engine displacement called out under the SS emblem on each front fender.

🢓 The Chevelle was considered an intermediate-sized car with a reasonable balance of proportions between the hood and trunk. The slightly smaller pony car classification generally refers to a long hood and short trunk, as these attributes are not shared with more pedestrian four-door sedans.

Additionally some of the 4,475 LS6 powerplants made their way into SS El Caminos. The exact number is unknown but can be estimated based on the total Malibu/ Chevelle SS production figures to be around 585 potential units. GMC also offered an El Camino pickup called the Sprint. Because the Sprint was not introduced until the 1971 model year, we can be certain that no LS6 GMC Sprints were ever sold to the public. The LS6 peaked in 1970 at 450 horsepower, only in the Chevelle SS. The M22 manual "Rock Crusher" transmission with Hurst shifter or the Turbo Hydramatic 400 automatic were the two mandatory options. Both were compatible with either the bucket seats and console or the standard bench seat. A Posi-Traction rear axle was not included with the LS6 engine and was a $42 option. Gear choices ranged from the standard 3.31:1 to a common choice of 4.10:1.

Driving the LS6 454 Chevelle is a visceral orchestrated concert, with the rhythmic tick of the mechanical lifters and high-lobe cam up front producing an even percussion from the rear of the car. The M22 four-speed manual transmission creates a musical whine as the RPMs increase, similar to the horns section coming in. Each component plays in harmony with the others, their sounds growing louder with the volume pedal on the floor, with sudden changes of octave between gears. The sounds finally peak as you cross the real or imaginary line and gently ease back off the throttle. All of this has occurred in just over 13.5 seconds and propelled you along with a 3,800-pound mixture of Detroit's best metal to a 108-mile-per-hour win.

The Chevrolet brass did not allow Corvettes access to the LS6 in 1970 but finally signed off on the combination for one year only in 1971. Without any promotion or fanfare, few buyers were aware of the option, with a mere 188 seizing the opportunity. Even with the compression ratio reduced to 9.0:1, the LS6 still provided 425 horsepower with 475 foot-pounds of torque. For this year the Chevelle SS was relegated to the LS5 454, with only 365 horsepower attributed to an anemic 8.5 to 1 compression ratio.

LS7: Over-the-Counter Engines

LATE IN 1970, Chevrolet introduced part #3965774, the 454 LS7 engine with 4.251-inch bore and 4.00-inch stroke. Equipped with solid valve lifters and a high-performance camshaft, it was available only as a "long-block" crated engine without the intake manifold, distributor, carb, water pump, or starter, all for a price of $1,497. This was a performance bargain, even in 1970 dollars. The engine included cast-iron rectangular port cylinder heads with 2.19 intake and 1.88 exhaust valves, heavy-duty 7/16 bolt-steel connecting rods, and special forged 12.25:1 compression pistons. It also featured a flat-tappet solid lifter cam with 560 intake and 600 exhaust lift, with a mechanical valve lash allowing for adjustment to maintain performance.

Chevrolet designed the LS7 454 beginning in late 1970 never placed it in any vehicles that were sold to the public. A writer for *Sports Car Graphic* magazine test-drove a single 1971 Corvette equipped with the LS7 engine. But because of the increase in insurance surcharges in the early 1970s and impending emissions standards, Chevrolet chose to use the engine only for off-road competition, although there was nothing to stop someone from replacing an existing big-block in a car and operating it on the street. Components, like the intake manifolds, were sold individually through GM's part departments.

The LS7 was an engine without a body. Built specifically for the Chevelle SS and Corvette chassis to win the horse-power-per-cubic-inch race, the 550-horsepower engine stuffed in a midsize car posed liabilities too great for even General Motors during the height of the horsepower wars. Instead, the choice of what to fit it in and how to use it was left to those owners who purchased the engine alone. One such owner chose to power the family car with a true LS7 spec motor back in the early 1970s. Dave Wulfsberg was racing a 1950 Chevrolet tin woody wagon that his father had bought new. After installing a series of small- and large-block Chevrolet powerplants, Dave read about the LS7 engine and inquired at his local dealership whether he could purchase one. Weeks later the engine arrived, and he immediately tore it apart to blueprint and fully balance the motor. Following the relatively easy process, he reassembled the new mill and replaced the old V-8 engine in the drag race family hauler.

Eventually he retired the wagon from the quarter mile. Dave removed and sold the LS7 and turned to a small-block for a more family-friendly cruiser.

⬆⬆ Chevrolet designers intended to produce a 1970 Chevelle SS with the factory LS7 465 horsepower sitting between the front frame rails. After corporate forbade this engine option, they chose to make it available as an over-the-counter crate engine. ⬅ Many of the LS7 engines were purchased and never installed in the project or race car they were slated for. This one was found and purchased in 2019 still untouched in its factory shipping crate. ⬈ The crated LS7 engine included specific warnings stating that the engine was designed for off-highway use only. Although released as a 1970 crated engine option, this part number remained in the factory part books throughout the 1970s.

It's obvious that the second-generation Camaro shared very little with the 1967–1969 models. In the eyes of many, it is one of the finest GM designs of the mid-century era.

↗↗ Because of strikes in the 1970 model year, General Motors delayed the introduction of the second-generation Camaro (and Firebird) from the fall of 1969 to the spring of 1970. This yellow coupe (the convertible was discontinued for 1970) is a rare Hurst Sunshine Special.

➡➡ The front and rear spoilers were unique to the Hurst Sunshine Special cars and were significantly larger than those found on the standard, Chevrolet-produced Z28 models. Before increasingly bigger bumpers were added, the 1970–1973 models are recognized as the purest expression of the second-generation Camaros.

WHEREAS THE BIG-BLOCK ENGINES were considered monster motors, the Z/28 350-cubic-inch V-8 was the mouse that roared. The LT1 motor was pulled directly from the Corvette product line as a 350 cubic-inch small-block rated at 360 horse-power but only 380 pounds-feet of torque. Sporting 11:1 compression, an aggressive high-lift solid cam, a lightweight aluminum intake, and a massive 750-cfm Holley carb, the exact same engine was rated at 370 horsepower with a 780-cfm Holley carb in the Corvette—a more expensive option in that model than the LS5 454 motor.

The new second-generation Camaro was tailored for a more European look with a lower center of gravity and improved handling. The Z/28 had dominated the Trans-Am racing circuit for the past three years, but competitors' designs were consistently im-proving. The lower stance, larger 15-inch wheels, and larger engine were also a distinct advantage on the street. The interior sported a redesigned dashboard with large, easy-to-read gauges and a wraparound cockpit. The lower profile was accomplished with a lowered roofline and the absence of rear quarter windows. Although it was marketed as a four-passenger coupe, your tall friends would need to leave their legs at home.

Introduced February 26, 1970, the Z/28 was a street competitor with large biceps. A total of 8,733 units made a production year shortened to six months. One major change from previous years' Z/28 offerings was that you could now get one with just two pedals and an automatic transmission.

The Z/28 Camaro was campaigned in the Trans-Am race series for the fourth year with a destroked 305-cubic-inch version of the LT1 engine, with only limited success—most likely from Chevrolet losing both its key driver, Mark Donohue, and the Penske organization to AMC, where they were winning with the new Javelin.

Camaro SS 396 L78

⬆ With only 2,464 units built, 1970 was the last year for the big-block Camaro. Camaro kept the tradition of identifying the big-block cars by painting the tail panel flat black.

UNLIKE THE CHEVELLE AND OTHER MIDSIZE General Motors cars that were built with a full frame, the Camaro was designed as a unibody with a front subframe. This design was both heavier and sturdier than the full unibody design utilized by the Ford, Chrysler, and AMC products.

In order to receive the big-block engine in the new 1970½ Camaro, you had to order the SS package. It was the last year for the L78 big-block rated at 375 horsepower. The 396 was actually a 402-cubic-inch engine that was an option for the SS package, which also included the F41 handling package with heavy-duty rear sway bar. Because the Camaro and the Nova did not have full-length frames, Chevrolet would not allow the largest, 454-cubic-inch motors to be factory-installed in these models. Muscle car builders Dick Harrell, Motion Performance, and Berger Chevrolet converted at least one unit each for the public. It appears that few, if any, others were built by the aftermarket shops for the 1970 model year. That may have been due to the late production release of the F-body Camaro or possibly because the same driver could walk into any Chevrolet showroom across America and drive away in a bonified monster LS6 454 Chevelle SS.

Total SS-package Camaro production was only 12,476, which included 10,012 four-barrel, 350-cubic-inch engines; 1,864 L34 350-horsepower, 396-cubic-inch engines; and a scant 600 of the L78 375-horsepower variety. All models could be had with the Turbo Hydra-matic automatic transmission.

A 1970 Camaro is easily distinguished from the other second-generation cars by its low-back bucket seats and low-profile rear decklid spoiler—replaced by a high-back Vega design and three-piece ducktail spoiler, respectively, the following year. Big-block cars would be called out on each front fender with 396 emblems and at the rear by the flat-black taillight panel.

Of the 124,901 Camaros built in 1970, 90 percent were V-8 models. Of those only 2,464 were ordered with the SS model with big-block engine. Although the 396 big-block option was continued for 1971, compression levels were dropped to 8.5:1, reducing horsepower to 300. All Camaro big block choices were discontinued after the 1971 model year.

◀◀ The new Camaro design created a more curvaceous and European look. The SS package and the Z-28 shared the new 15-inch Rally wheel design. This car also sports the split bumper and extended grille of the Rally Sport option.

◀ The interior of the 1970 Camaro included a wraparound gauge panel, creating a cockpit experience for the driver.

◀ The big block 396 (402) engine filled the pony car's engine bay. Air conditioning was available on the 350-horsepower L34 option but was excluded when the L78 375-horsepower engine was installed.

⬆ The Nova was the lowest-cost Chevrolet for 1970, and most were built for basic transportation. When the Super Sport option was chosen, the buyer had the choice of multiple V-8 engines including the 375-horsepower 396.

CHEVROLET'S SMALLEST ECONOMY CAR had officially changed its name from Chevy II to Nova, but customers could still purchase it with a thrifty four-cylinder, 230-cubic-inch engine producing just 140 horsepower. For those who wanted a better power/economy balance, the more common choice was the 250-cubic-inch six-cylinder. The low-priced model came complete with taxicab interior with rubber floor mats, remaining totally devoid of luxuries. The last year for both the little four-cylinder and the big-block in the Nova was 1970.

Because the Nova was not a full-frame car, it was officially limited by corporate rules to a 400-cubic-inch engine, although technically the 396 measured out at 402 cubic inches.

The Nova was smaller and less sporty than the Chevelle and was intentionally limited to two body styles for the 1970 model year. Redesigned in 1968 from the previous boxy configuration, it incorporated a semifastback look in both the two-door and four-door models. No hardtop or wagon versions were offered, but the car was could carry six adults in some semblance of comfort with the full-width front and back bench seats.

The Nova was not a first thought in the muscle-car market, and Chevrolet intentionally limited its option choices as well. If a buyer was looking for something more luxurious or sporty, dealers had the Malibu/Chevelle models or even the sportier Camaro ready for a test drive.

But there was one hidden option package for the Nova. It was seldom promoted, and when it did appear in advertising, it was generally along with other, more profitable performance models. To the untrained eye, the Super Sport package did not even change a Nova's appearance. Externally the SS package for 1970 provided a blacked-out grille with an *SS* center badge and a full-width, 4-inch-tall ribbed tail-panel molding also stating *SS*. Lower rocker moldings and two fake air vents centered on the trailing edge of the hood were similar to the 1967–1968 Camaro. Both front fenders bore 350 or 396 block number callouts just above the side marker lights as well as two vertical ribbed vents attached to the trailing sides in front of the doors. There were no bold stripe options like the Chevelle SS or Camaro Z/28 received for 1970. The package was subtle, and the Nova became the sleeper of Chevrolet's performance offerings.

Just over a quarter million Novas were manufactured in 1970. Of those only 19,558 were ordered with the SS package powered with either the 350-cubic-inch or the 396-cubic-inch engine. Just 3,765 buyers, or 1.5 percent, chose the highest-horsepower L78 mechanical lifter motor. The potential magic in the Nova emerged from a power-to-weight analysis. Chevrolet recognized this, and although it never allowed the powerful 454 V-8 in the lighter subframe cars, it did offer the potent 396-cubic-inch 375-horsepower motor with optional L89 aluminum heads. The weight savings of replacing the cast heads and intake with aluminum was about 200 pounds. Keeping in mind that this weight was trimmed from the front and the top, every pound removed created a traction advantage at the drag strip during launch due to the physics of

⬇ Finding an accurately-restored 1970 big block Nova is a difficult task with only 3,765 units produced out of almost 250,000 Novas that year.

weight transfer. This diet produced an enticing 3,400-pound curb weight for a downright provocative 9 pounds per horsepower. The SS package was offered only in one body style, the stout two-door post sedan complete with vent windows.

There have been many more big-block Novas made by subsequent owners than Chevrolet ever assembled in 1970. Only 5,567 buyers chose to purchase the big-block Nova for this year. It is estimated that 1,802 were the basic 360-horsepower L34, with the other two-thirds of buyers (3,765) opting for the mighty 375-horsepower L78. While they were great at the strip, they were practically invisible on the street given their absence of flash. Even the semifastback design was hidden, as both the four-door senior citizen version and the two-door sedan shared the same silhouette.

The body plate will designate only whether the car was original with a six-cylinder or V-8 engine, but there are a few ways to tell whether a Nova came from the factory with a big-block engine. It must be an SS, as no big-block cars came without that package. Power front disc brakes were a mandatory option for all SS Novas. The heater core cover on the passenger side of the firewall will have a distinct relief in it to clear the back of the passenger side big-block head. Dual exhaust hanger points will be present on all original SS cars.

Although you could get a 350-cubic-inch V-8 in a standard Nova, only the SS package provided both four-barrel carb and dual exhaust. Most SS package cars also were adorned with the 14×7 Magnum 500 rally wheels painted in silver and charcoal with detachable trim rings.

Both the engine and transmission were serial numbered to the car. If the original drivetrain is missing, verifying the original horsepower rating will be difficult. Locating an original 396-cubic-inch, 375-horsepower Nova is difficult. Only an original build sheet or documentation will identify whether the car received the

➡ The standard Nova interior was all business. Many were built with rubber floor coverings and bench seats. If your goal was to go fast for as little money as possible, the Nova fit that bill. Carpets, bucket seats, and consoles were available if you so desired and were willing to pony up the extra coins.

350-horsepower 396 or the 375-horsepower engine. If you can verify that the car came with a big-block, there's a two-out-of-three chance it started with the mechanical-lifter 375-horsepower motor.

The interior can be as sparse as a 1960s taxicab or a little sporty in appearance. Neither a deluxe steering wheel nor tilt was an option. The standard gauge package included a wide, nondescript speedometer with a fuel gauge and idiot lights and an empty area to the right for an optional clock or small tachometer. When the car was ordered with bucket seats, buyers could also include an optional floor console that had four small (hard-to-read) gauges in a pod at the front under the dash. These replaced the dash warning lights with amp, coolant temp, oil pressure, and fuel.

Despite Chevrolet's half-hearted efforts to market the model, word got out. The 3,500-pound Nova performed well at the track with quarter-mile times in the low 14 seconds and top speeds of 105 miles per hour. Traction was a limiting factor unless the rear wheel openings were enlarged to accommodate a larger wheel-tire combination.

An additional 177 Novas were ordered under the COPO program and marketed as the Yenko Deuce with the Z/28 350-cubic-inch LT1 engine. Yenko was unprepared for the success of this spring-released specialty car and reached out for assistance from Hurst Performance, which helped assemble 50 of these units.

Although the big-block Nova had a strong following, the LS6 454 Chevelle SS was the undisputed pinnacle of Chevrolet's high-performance muscle car offerings. Almost 4,500 car buyers stepped up and testified to this fact with their hard-earned dollars. Many of the well-optioned versions of this car had a window sticker approaching the $6,000 mark—clearly into Corvette territory and almost double the cost of the midyear "package" cars offered the year before. The rule of "You can go as fast as you can afford" became the motto of the muscle car wars.

◄ The Chevrolet Novas had a long list of creature comfort options that increased the window sticker cost to nearly that of a similarly-equipped Chevelle or Camaro. For this reason, high option Nova SS models are hard to find today.

Ford and Mercury

The 1970 Ford offerings were mostly carryover from the many new models introduced in 1969, including the top-dog Boss 429 created for the sole purpose of competing against the NASCAR-dominating Hemi-powered Dodges and Plymouths. Chevrolet had removed itself from factory-sponsored racing in 1963, leaving Ford and Chrysler in a heated competition that packed grandstands across the nation as NASCAR came of age in the 1960s.

Ford's performance offerings were a smorgasbord. Many consumers were easily confused by the different packages and names. Most were directly connected to the Mustang model line. Choices included Sport Coupe, Fastback, GT, Cobra, Mach 1, Drag Pack, Shelby GT350, Shelby GT500, Cobra Jet (CJ), Grande, Boss, and Super Cobra Jet (SCJ). (Mustang for the 1970 model year, the GT badge was dropped from the Mustang except on Shelby models, although it continued on the midsize Torino line.) Ford Performance engine-displacement choices were no less confusing. Ford offered passenger-car V-8 engines in the 302, Boss 302, 351 Windsor (all small-blocks), 351 Cleveland, 390, 428, 428 CJ, 428 Police Interceptor, 429, 429 CJ, 429 SCJ, and don't forget the Boss 429 in both NASCAR (T for track) and street (S) configuration.

Ford Mustang 428 CJ and SCJ with Drag Pack

Mercury Cougar 428 SCJ

Ford Boss 429 Mustang

Ford Torino Cobra 429 SCJ

Mercury Cyclone Spoiler 429 SCJ

Mercury Cougar Eliminator

Even ram-air and non-ram-air engines used unique designations. A ram-air 428 CJ was an R-code; without ram air, the same engine was displayed in the VIN of the car with a Q-code. Similarly, the standard 429 Thunder Jet was an N code, the 429 CJ non–ram air was a C-code, and with ram air, the 429 CJ became a J-code. These fine-grained VIN designations allow for a clear understanding of how a car was built from the factory, as most of these high-performance cars were raced and altered over the years. Many muscle cars became derelict over the years with engines and body parts removed for other projects. As values of restored examples have increased, cars that weren't worth the effort twenty years ago now have increased in value, particularly when restored to original configuration.

Another great asset to the Ford restoration process is Marti Auto Works. Kevin Marti's business has contracted with Ford Motor Company to access the Ford and Mercury database to authenticate production documents for cars built between 1967 and 2017. Acquiring a Marti Report on any rare Ford is a requirement to authenticate how the car was ordered from the factory as well as what options it had and what the rarity of the combined components equates to today. While this service will not be able to identify how many similar Fords have survived today, each model tends to have a hobby-driven registry to assist in estimating these numbers. Marti Auto Works is not able to provide information on cars manufactured before the 1967 model year due to the loss of Ford records to fire in 1970.

With high-performance cars receiving a surcharge based on the previous year's ratings, changes in nomenclature could help with insurance costs, at least until the underwriters had a chance to catch up, although Ford became a competitor to itself with all the overlapping versions of the Mustang platform. With all of the Ford engine options and configurations, it can take an expert to clearly define the lineage of each performance package, its origins, and its offspring. In this case, we consulted with known Ford and Mercury expert Bill Basore, who has helped clarify the history of these Ford offerings for 1970.

SPECIAL-PACKAGE MUSTANGS

Ford had learned that options created additional profit for each car manufactured. When the Mustang was first introduced, it was designed to be affordable and cover a wide expanse of the consumer's needs. From a basic mode of transportation to a high-performance sports car, the Mustang appealed to a vast array of buyer preferences. In 1965 Ford had a difficult time keeping up with demand and had to question the wisdom of working so hard at building a basic low-profit car when the same efforts could produce a more profitable unit.

The automaker released two packages in the spring of 1965 to help the consumer choose to spend more money with a single decision to upgrade. Both the Pony interior package and the GT performance package helped increase the average sales price of the Mustang. By 1966 even the six-cylinder Mustang had received an upgrade in the Sprint package, which included the larger six-cylinder option, automatic transmission, console, and chrome engine dress-up.

This process was fully entrenched for the 1969 and 1970 model years and became the method for selling multiple versions of the Mustang and other muscle-car bodies. The Mach 1, Boss, Grande, and Shelby packages ensured that specific options were included and that Ford made an additional profit on each unit while also building an image to the youthful buyer. Similarly the different high-performance engine options either included or required additional performance components to handle the added torque and horsepower. The bottom line for any manufacturer was profit, and by 1970 the muscle-car industry had learned that a favorable performance image was more profitable than providing basic and reliable transportation.

The base-model Mustangs could be carefully optioned to create an all-business racer for those seeking function over form, knowing that options add weight and weight is the enemy. The Mach 1 was for the knowledgeable street racer who knew which boxes to check to end up with a formidable performance car that included both comfort and style. The Shelby was for the more mature consumer looking to stand out with a new sleeker appearance tied into the famous Shelby name and the characteristic sequential taillights. Lastly there was the Boss 429 buyer, hunting for maximum muscle designed to win the NASCAR championship at all costs. This was the most expensive choice and the least practical for everyday use, as it was a brute to drive, devoid of many of the creature comforts built into the other offerings.

⬆ A 429 mill is lowered into a 1969 Mustang on the Kar Kraft assembly line.

FORD BIG-BLOCK ENGINE HISTORY

In 1962 Ford introduced the 406 FE block casting, which moved the bores further apart than on the 390 V-8 but over time exhibited a weak bottom end. Ford reduced this issue by improving the strength with a cross-bolt design. The 427 was developed from a stroked 406 and was the engine that eventually went to and won Le Mans.

Ford was still running the 427 engine for NASCAR when the second-generation Chrysler 426 Hemi engine was introduced to the public at Daytona in 1964. Street versions of the Hemi appeared in very limited numbers for the 1966 model year. Due to the 427's restrictive valve design, Ford was not able to compete with the Hemi. Its solution was to build an overhead cam 427 engine rated at 685 horsepower. Ford built five hundred 427-cubic-inch overhead-cam motors but never put one in a car

body offered to the public, even though it was capable of being detuned for practical street driving.

The solution came from performance-oriented Tasca Ford in Providence, Rhode Island, which was not happy with the performance of the new 1967 Mustang GT 390 notchback it was drag racing. The 390's restrictive stock valve configuration was giving the jump to its direct competitor, the 1967 Camaro with the L/8 396-cubic-inch, 375-horsepower engine. Tasca technician Billy Loomis replaced the 390 with a 428 Police Interceptor, swapped in racing heads from a Ford 406 motor, and fitted a lightweight dual four-barrel intake. With that engine and some suspension upgrades, Tasca started winning races. Its success caught the public's attention—and *Hot Rod* magazine's, when the Tasca Mustang ran a best of 13.39 at 105 miles per hour.

Ford Mustang 428 CJ and SCJ with Drag Pack

⬆ Flamboyant colors became more popular in the early 1970s. This Mach 1 Mustang is painted Grabber Blue and sports the 428 Cobra Jet engine with the factory shaker ram air hood scoop.

FOR 1970 FORD RESTYLED the Mustang in a few obvious ways. Gone was the unusual four-headlamp design with two outboard headlights and two in the grille. The new look revived the trademark two-headlight configuration, but through striking the outer lights from 1969. The grille was widened and the headlights kept in the grille opening. Around back the concave rear taillight panel was painted flat black with flush-mounted taillights. The traditional three vertically mounted taillights remained, only mounted in deep recesses compared to the previous year's stand out lights.

Hot Rod tested the Tasca Ford Mustang race car and decided to push Ford into building the combined engine components so that Tasca (and others) could legally race in the stock class. Leveraging the subscribers of the magazine, Eric Dahlquist wrote an article and asked people to write to Henry Ford II. The article came complete with a prelabeled coupon to send to the Deuce. He soon found his desk covered with these little postcards, and the fix was in.

Released by midyear 1968 as the Cobra Jet Mustang with just 1,299 units made, this combination was soon dominating drag strips across North America. This Cobra Jet engine was also used by Shelby in the late production run of 1,570 1968 GT500 KRs alongside the GT500 models built with the standard Thunder Jet 360-horsepower, 428-cubic-inch powerplant. Even with the hefty additional horsepower, the big-block did not bring a lot of advantage in the quarter mile over the lighter GT350 with the 271-horsepower Hi-Po 289 due to the GT500's massive engine weight.

First introduced midyear 1968 in the Mustang and the Shelby offerings, the 428 CJ would become standard in the 1969–1970 Shelby GT500s. The Mach 1 trim package was introduced in 1969 and was available only with the fastback SportsRoof body. You could also purchase the Q-code 428 CJ engine without the ram-air option in a Mustang hardtop, SportsRoof, or even convertible, all without the Mach 1 package.

The Super Cobra Jet package arose when the 428 Cobra Jet was factory-ordered with the optional 3.91 or 4.30 rear axle ratio. The ratio was designated on the driver's door as either a V or W respectively; ordering either of these axles automatically upgraded the 428 Cobra Jet to the SCJ status. Picking the 3.91 or 4.30 rear end also meant that factory air-conditioning was no longer available. The SCJ included upgraded 427-style connecting rods and upgraded harmonic balancer. Together this package was introduced in midyear 1969 as the Drag Pack. All Drag Pack cars received the 428 SCJ engine upgrade. Both 428 CJ versions were available with the optional ram-air

⬇ Even factory big-block muscle cars came with wheel covers. This Mach 1 is adorned with the one-year-only 1970 simulated mag-style wheel covers, which were standard for this model.

⬇⬇ The rear angle shows the Mach 1 name boldly spelled out on the trunk lid. The black tail panel, stripe, and name helped distinguish the powerful Mach 1 from the more standard SportsRoof models. The side received a stylish lower body cladding that continued the Mach 1 theme.

⬇ Although the Cobra Jet name was visible to the driver sitting next to you at a stop light, the 428 callout remained difficult to see.

⬇⬇ The ram air assembly remains attached to the engine and seals to the hole in the factory hood. By being fixed to the motor, the hood scoop would shake and move with each blip of the throttle. This movement lead to the shaker name for this hood scoop design.

package, which included the shaker hood scoop sitting atop an open-element air cleaner. The ram-air option increased the factory horsepower rating from 335 to 360. The more accurate rating would have been closer to 400 horsepower. A factory-equipped 428 SCJ Mustang would break into the high 13-second quarter-mile time range on standard bias-ply wide oval tires.

Ford made sure that the average consumer was knowledgeable about the CJ/SCJ engine option on the Mustang. In August 1968 it had released over twenty 428 CJ–powered Mach 1 model press cars to get the word out; most of these were red with similar equipment used for marketing and new car-show purposes. For 1970 the big-block Mustangs were again prominently displayed both at newsstands and in showrooms. Resulting interest prompted 21,492 R-code 428 CJ/SCJ Mustang and Shelby orders over 1969 and 1970. In 1970 only 137 buyers ordered a Cobra Jet engine option in a Mustang convertible, although there were no R-code Grandes produced in 1969 or 1970. Fewer than 20 of those were R-code 428 Cobra Jet cars with four-speed transmission complete with the shaker hood scoop ram-air package. Even with the strong sales and competitive success of the 428 Mustang, it was gone for 1971, replaced with the one-year-only 429 CJ and SCJ versions.

In 1968 Ford introduced a new motor that would later be called the DOVE engine, introduced as the 429 Thunder Jet. A new head design being developed for this engine was originally referred to as the blue crescent; it finally incorporated the canted valve design creating a crescent-shaped combustion chamber with the spark plug placed in the middle. The following year this would become the Boss 429 block with hemi-style heads.

This engine family would play a part in the longer 1971 Mustang hood designed to accommodate the large 429 engine. Ford even had expectations of larger motors, up to 500 cubic inches, being developed from this same block. When Iacocca took control of Ford in 1970, he chose to focus on the smaller-car market and slated the Mustang for eventual downsizing to a version of the Pinto chassis.

⬆ The 1970 Mach 1 interior is plush and comfortable. The Hurst shifter juts out of the factory console for a driver's easy reach.

THE COUGAR SHARED the same platform, Dearborn assembly line, and drivetrain components as the Mustang. Mercury's creativity was limited to the Cat's aesthetics and marketing. In previous years the XR7 had been a Mercury counterpart to Mustang's GT packages, the difference being that the Mustang GT was primarily performance based, while the XR7 was more an upscale interior package. For 1969 both Ford and Mercury expanded the package choices to include the Mach 1 and the Eliminator, both of which had a true performance vibe without the bare-knuckled approach that the Boss 302 and Boss 429 offered. An educated Mercury consumer would see that all the performance options offered on the Mach 1 Mustang were also available for the Cougar.

Although the standard Cougar engine for 1970 was the 351-2V, Cougars could be had with almost any Ford V-8 motor that year. Unlike its sibling, the Cougar was never offered with a four-cylinder engine. Marketing felt the Mercury brand was more upscale and that the Cougar buyer was more sophisticated than the average Ford buyer. Marketing and promotional photography reflected this with upscale clothing, older-looking drivers, and more expensive neighborhoods and other backdrops. The result was an image for the car that appealed more to women than to men. Although women were a growing market force for new-car buyers in the late 1960s, most purchases were still heavily influenced by a male companion or family member.

⬆ The Cougar's front end had a more aggressive look in 1970. The beaked nose hides a small vertical grille that helps keep the big 428-cubic-inch Cobra Jet engine cool.

By 1970 the Cougar marketing team had expanded the brand's image to include the young male buyer. The Eliminator package included the requisite scoops, stripes, and spoilers backed up by Ford's big-block offerings of 390 and 428 cubic inches. The latter was not just any 428 motor, like what had offered in previous years' full-size Montereys and Marauders, but the 428 Cobra Jet that was winning drag races across North America.

The Cougar in 1970 had minor appearance changes over the previous year's model. The most significant difference was the front end's move from 1969's wall-to-wall grille to a split design similar to the 1967–1968 models. The painted section that dropped down from the hood was nicknamed the "tooth" grille in relation to the Cougar badge. The Eliminator package included blacked-out grilles on each side of the body-color tooth. The tooth would become the starting point of the flat-black stripe that ascended the hood and tucked under the flat-black Ram-Air scoop on the 428 CJ models.

⬆ The 1970 Mercury Cougar Eliminator had body-color appointments such as this factory spoiler. The following year the spoiler was flat black, regardless of the body color of the car.

◤◤ The Cougar Eliminator gauge package is large and easy to read. The open area of the steering wheel ensures the driver can easily keep track of the drivetrain's vital functions.

Ford Boss 429 Mustang

BUNKIE KNUDSEN MOVED from General Motors to Ford in 1969 with full knowledge of GM's future product offerings. Even with this competitive advantage, he found himself helpless to steer Ford management away from their projected small-car product schedule, as Ford's product plans for 1969 and 1970 were already firmly locked in place.

He brought along from GM young designer Larry Shinoda, who was quickly tasked with creating a more track-ready competitor out of the Mustang. Shinoda's plan was to develop two cars, one based on the 302-cubic-inch small-block for Trans-Am racing and another as a way to homologate the larger semihemi 429-cubic-inch engine to compete in NASCAR. Because Shinoda referred to Knudsen as "boss," which also was a positive term with young people, this would soon become the attention-getting name for both versions of the Mustang.

The Boss 429 engine was the ultimate evolution of the Ford 385 engine. The 385 name came from the design's 3.85-inch crankshaft stroke. The design also featured four-bolt main caps and forged-steel crank and connecting rods.

To save weight the engine was created with aluminum cylinder heads. Although referred to as a hemi design, it had a semihemispherical or crescent-shaped combustion chamber. The design precluded the engine coolant from the block from going directly through a head gasket into the heads. The heads were sealed to the block with passages fitted with industrial-style O-rings similar to diesel or racing engines.

⬆ All Mustangs got a mild restyling in 1970. The biggest change came up front, where a single high/low beam headlight integrated into the grille replaced quad headlights.

Due to the need for an individual seal around each liquid opening, there were twenty-one separate O-rings for sealing the oil and coolant passages. Combustion surfaces still utilized a traditional head gasket design between the iron block and aluminum heads. For the first year, the Boss 429 used a dual exhaust system with separate exhaust pipes and resonators that combined into a single traverse-mounted cross-flow muffler, then separated into dual exhaust exits.

The 1969 Boss 429 came with two different designations, T for track (580 units) and S for street (279 units). T-engine cars received the mechanical lifters and lighter weight rods to allow the 429 cubic inches to breathe. The S engines used a hydraulic camshaft and heavier connecting rods, each weighing close to 3 pounds. Ford Performance published a letter informing owners of a mechanical camshaft upgrade that Ford claimed provided an additional 25 horsepower, which resulted in a quarter-mile time reduced by 1 second and a trap seed increased by 5 miles per hour.

The 1970 Boss 429 had significant changes to improve the owner experience. Hydraulic lifters were gone, replaced by solid lifters, which many believe improved the performance. The exhaust design now included two separate pipes and mufflers, and all Boss motors received an electronic rev limiter that interrupted ignition over 5,800 rpm. Both years the Boss 429 engine came standard with a single 735-cfm Holley four-barrel carburetor mounted on a free-flowing aluminum intake manifold to meet the mandatory federal emission standards. Ford was forced to install the Thermactor pollution-control system on every Boss 429 sold to the public. Most of these air-pump systems were removed as soon as the one-year warranty had expired.

⬇ The Boss 429 version followed the styling of other Mustangs with the signature three-element taillight that traces back to the first Mustangs that hit showrooms in the spring of 1964.

There were no attention-grabbing stripes for this special car; the only identification was the *Boss 429* decal on each front fender. The oversized air scoop was sealed to the top of the air cleaner and manually controlled by a knob under the dash. Another major change for 1970 was the choice of interior colors: a white interior was available in place of the standard black comfort-weave seats. Additionally all 1970 Boss 429s had the hood scoop finished in flat black as compared to body color.

The basic SportsRoof Mustang retailed for $2,872. Adding the Boss 429 engine package bumped up the price by $1,208 and triggered the mandatory options of four-speed, Drag Pack, competition suspension, tachometer, power front disc brakes, and power steering, adding another $659 for a total minimum cost of $4,739. If you added in AM radio, deluxe interior group, console, and freight, most "Boss Nine" owners spent just under $5,000 new.

Kar Kraft was a Ford skunkworks partner in Brighton, Michigan, that enabled Ford's Special Vehicles engineers to create low-volume production runs of cars not possible to build on Ford's regular production lines. The Mustang's standard engine compartment was not wide enough to accommodate the Boss 429 engine's width, so to create space, Ford designed new inner shock-tower aprons that were installed on the River Rouge Mustang assembly line. Ford also installed reworked front fenders with a slightly larger radius due to rolling the factory lip. The Kar Kraft team changed the front suspension shock towers, resulting in the lower A-arms moving 0.5 inch outward and the upper A-arms dropping a full inch. They also installed the trunk-mounted battery and heavy-duty ¾-inch rear sway bar to help the nose-heavy Mustang handle.

Only 499 1970 Boss 429s made it through the Kar Kraft production line, compared to 857 in the half-year production in 1969. Even with an average cost of over $5,000, Ford probably lost money on every car built and chose to stop production at the 500 units required to homologate the Boss 429 for NASCAR. Either Ford fudged on the count submitted to NASCAR or it included the few prototypes built that were not sold to the public. With limited color and option choices, the Boss 429 proved to be memorable when you saw one in person, but it was a better track car than a daily driver. Most were promptly relegated to special events and therefore retained low mileage due to the impracticality of driving a car that achieved miles per gallon only in the single digits.

⬆ This is one of the high-water marks of Ford's Total Performance era: the Boss 429 V-8. For 1970 Ford's outsourced builder, Kar Kraft, was able to stuff 429-cubic-inch cammers under the hoods of 499 Mustangs Boss 429s.

⬆⬆ For 1970, Ford offered the choice of a heavy-duty Cruise-O-Matic three-speed automatic or, as in this case, a close-ratio four-speed manual.

Shelby Mustangs: The GT350 and GT500

THE 1969 SHELBY GT500 was a Mustang 428 CJ in a smoking jacket. Carroll Shelby terminated his agreement with Ford in summer 1969, essentially killing his personal association with the Mustang line for the next thirty-five years. For two years Ford had been in control of Shelby design, construction, and marketing. In the crowd of Mustang performance offerings the Shelby needed to be differentiated from the other models. The distinctive and longer fiberglass Shelby nose was adapted from the 1967 Mach 1 show car and hinted at what the Mustang would look like with the 1971 refresh.

Although the basic Shelby received the same drivetrain and related components while being assembled alongside the other Mustangs on the Dearborn line, the real transformation was conducted at the upfitter company, A. O. Smith, in Livonia, Michigan. Ford had contracted with A. O. Smith starting in 1968 to convert the Mustang into a Shelby offsite without interrupting Ford's assembly line. Shelby production and sales would peak in 1968 with 4,450 units produced.

Ford separated the Shelby and Cobra names in 1969. Although the Cobra Jet motor nomenclature was retained, the Shelby Cobra association was severed. Ford had started badging the Fairlane as a Cobra in 1968. By 1970 Ford used the Torino Cobra name for the 429 CJ and SCJ package cars.

For 1969 the Shelby was surrounded by Mustang-based competitors. Buyers had a wide choice of models right in the local Ford showroom. They could order their 428-cubic-inch engine wrapped in a variety of sheet metal or fiberglass clothing. These options started with a base-model Mustang in all three body configurations, the Mach 1 in the SportsRoof body, the Shelby in the convertible or SportsRoof, or even the Boss 429 in SportsRoof body. All of these choices were separated by subtle imaging and advertising position. With a sticker price up to $5,400, the Shelby GT500 was more expensive than any other Mustang-based performance car in 1970.

Orders for the 1969 model year dropped by about 30 percent, to 3,150 Shelby GT350 and GT500 models, with an additional 601 produced but remaining unsold. There were only a few minor differences between a 1969 and a 1970 Shelby. The engine received an updated distributor and an altered carburetor, including a new carburetor tag stamped *ED* for "edited." The most obvious external differentiation was two black paint stripes added on the hood, starting at the two outside NACA scoops and terminating at the rear of the hood. The second way to identify a 1970-model Shelby is to look for the added lower front air-dam spoiler. The spoiler was not factory-installed due to potential damage during shipping but was included in the trunk for dealer installation.

The last change required replacement of the factory Autolite carburetor to meet 1970 federal emissions requirements. These changes were made through a new contract with A. O. Smith under the watchful eye of the Federal Bureau of Investigation. The leftover units would be carried over into the 1970 production year due to a re-VIN procedure again witnessed and documented by the FBI. This was the only time the FBI oversaw the VIN change procedure for a US-manufactured vehicle. One change that would be needed for any cars produced after January 1, 1970, was a locking ignition key built into the steering column that was not part of the 1969 model build. Ford had to finish the Shelby renumbering process before the new year to remain in compliance with federal traffic safety rules.

For 1970, the last time the Shelby name was attached to a US-built Mustang two-doors, both a GT350 (351 cubic inch) and GT500 (428 Cobra Jet) were offered. They can be distinguished from the 1969 models built off of the same body shell by the addition of two black stripes on the hood and the black front chin spoiler.

↑ The new-for-1970 intermediate-sized Torino body projected a look that was both svelte and muscular. The long nose and fastback roofline gave the car an aerodynamic appearance that did not translate to the banked oval track.

TECHNICALLY THERE NEVER WAS a Ford Torino Cobra in 1970. There were the Falcon, Torino, Torino GT, Ranchero, and Cobra, all based on the Torino midsize body. Ford had increased the dimensions of the Torino line for 1970, creating a very attractive and sporty look to replace the boxy design of previous years. Ford also chose to abandon the Fairlane designation after fifteen years in favor of the more European name Torino, the local name for Turin, Italy.

The new design accomplished two major goals for Ford in 1970. First, it had a larger engine compartment specifically engineered to accept the larger 429 engine that wouldn't fit in the previous year's model. Ford was moving away from the FE-based 390 and 428 engines and wanted to standardize on the larger 429 blocks, which were expected to grow up to 500 cubic inches in displacement. Second, the new Torino was the choice for NASCAR, with more aerodynamic styling vitally needed for a successful racing season.

Although the performance goal was centered around the swoopy two-door fastback, the Torino platform helped Ford fill many body configurations needed for the growing midsize market. There were a total of eight different body styles totaling twelve different branded offerings on this platform—two-door post, two-door semifastback, full fastback (SportsRoof), convertible, Ranchero pickup, four-door post sedan, four-door brougham hardtop, and station wagon. Ford invested heavily to overcome the shortcomings that the Talladega and Cyclone Spoiler attempted to correct in 1969, believing the new Torino would command more market share alongside its full-size Galaxie/LTD line.

Once again Ford offered a confusing smorgasborg of performance engine choices for the Torino and Cobra models. A buyer had a choice of three 429-cubic-inch motors with very close horsepower ratings: the N-code 429 Thunder Jet (not CJ) engine rated at 360 horsepower; the C-code 429 CJ non–ram air rated at 370 horsepower; or the king-of-the-hill J-code ram air with the 429 CJ rated at 375 horsepower.

A Torino ordered with either the C- or N-code 429 engine could be a sleeper without the attention-getting shaker hood scoop or even a flat-black hood. For one year only, the Ford Falcon shared the Torino platform. This lightweight two-door post could be ordered with either of the 429 CJ engines, making it a formidable competitor. The last year of the Falcon, it was only available with the bare-bones two-door post sedan or the four-door post sedan. Most Falcons were ordered as basic transportation with the 200-cubic-inch six-cylinder engine, but if you come across one of the fifteen or so 429 models, do not race against it for pink slips. Ford also built a few of the 429 CJ versions of the Ranchero GT, although none were officially available in the Torino station wagon for 1970 (although a few may have been authorized as special orders).

Knowing it was the largest engine available in a midsize Ford, you would think that more buyers would opt for the massive 429 in either standard, Cobra Jet, or Super Cobra Jet trim. The public and the press both loved the new Torino, with *Motor Trend* awarding it Car of the Year honors. Sales numbers were 50% greater than the previous year. The Torino GT tended to be ordered with more creature comforts than the Torino Cobra, which was more like muscles on steroids. The small number of 429 orders could be attributed to the rising insurance rates and the multitude of performance model choices each buyer could consider under the Ford umbrella.

⬇ This low angle shows an angular design with a slightly recessed grille. Cobra package cars came with optional 15-inch chrome Magnum 500 wheels.

The true fastback body used for the Cobra and Torino GT models has a lower roofline than its two-door hardtop sibling. None of the glass is shared between the true fastback and the other two-door hardtop versions of this platform. To help differentiate the fastback (body code 38) known as the SportsRoof in Ford's marketing materials, from the semifastback, the Cobra had a higher deck lid with two black insert panels on the drop side of the trunk that was very similar to the tail light panel used on the Mach 1 Mustangs.

Because of this rear deck design, Ford mounted the rear spoiler on two pedestals that were not allowed to be factory-ordered on the fastback models. Cobra models were further distinguished by the blacked-out hood center with the optional shaker ram air scoop and dual twist hood locks. Each Torino model so equipped received a 429 emblem mounted low on each front fender between the wheel and the front door. If the car was the Cobra package, it also received a Cobra name and stylized snake with flaming mag wheels in place of the snake coil. The outside received a few distinctive touches with optional rear window slats similar to those offered on the Boss 302 as well as an optional laser side stripe that started in one color on each front fender and faded into another reminiscent of a hippie's tie-dyed shirt.

The interior received a refresh with a dashboard layout that you would expect to find in a typical family station wagon family station wagon. Ford settled by providing idiot lights where performance gauges should have been. The dash is mostly consumed by a wide, nondescript 120-mile-per-hour speedometer. If you opted for the factory tachometer it came as a hard-to-read ribbon that rolled behind a stationary line rather than a traditional sweeping arrow that could be easily glanced at to determine the rpm count. Additionally, it was tucked into the small rectangle to the left of the speedometer.

➡ Although the literature specified the Cobra as its own model, the hood still identified the car as a Torino. Twist lock hood pins and black-out treatment were all part of the Cobra package.

Many Cobras can be found with aftermarket tachometers strapped to the steering column for a more consistent shift point.

The Cyclone Spoiler, which was the Mercury version of the Cobra, incorporated factory gauges missing from the Ford in the dash pad to the right of the speedometer. Although those gauges were more toward the center of the car, they were mounted high and angled toward the driver. The Torino GT and Cobra seating options ranged from a bench front seat with an automatic transmission on the steering column to a floor-mounted Hurst shifter in a console between comfortable high-back bucket seats.

The base engine offering in the Torino Cobra was the 10.5:1 compression N-code 429 with an Autolite four-barrel carburetor, cast-iron two-bolt mains in the block, and hydraulic lifters, rated at 360 horsepower. The next option was the C-code 429 Cobra Jet, based on the same basic engine design with improved heads that had smaller combustion chambers. The combination along with larger valves increased the compression ratio to 11.3:1. This increased performance added $164 to the bill and 10 horsepower to the rating (370) and included a larger 700-cfm Rochester Quadrajet atop a different intake manifold. This engine was designed to be more efficient breathing air, but at a cost of 30 foot-pounds of torque. The added horsepower remained stealthy under the long, flat Cobra hood.

If you wanted the ram-air option via the shaker hood scoop, it would add $229 and change the engine designation to a J code. The ram-air option was rated to provide a measly 5-horsepower gain, but those who read the spec sheets and the press reviews knew that Ford was intentionally trying to deceive the sanctioning bodies of racing and the insurance underwriters. If you really knew what you were looking for, you would also check off the Drag Pack option that included either 3.91 or 4.30 rear Traction-Lok. The dealer brochure wouldn't tell you, but selecting that one little option changed most everything in the driveline from the radiator back. The engine was now a hefty four-bolt main version of the 429 with forged-aluminum pistons and an aggressive solid-lifter camshaft, although still (under)rated at 375 horsepower and still showing a J-code designation in the VIN. To keep this venomous snake cool it also received an external oil cooler mounted up by the radiator and a power-steering cooler mounted on the front of the block. A Holley 4150-series carburetor rated at 780 cfm mixed air and fuel beneath the shaker hood scoop. The 429 required either the four-speed manual top loader or heavy-duty C6 automatic transmission.

The Cobra package also included a heavy-duty front sway bar, power front disc brakes, optional 15x7 chrome Magnum 500 wheels, and raised-white-letter F60×15 Firestone Wide Oval tires. When so equipped, it was a solid 13-second car straight from the factory. Those quarter-mile times put it in the category of the big-block LS6 Chevelle SS454 or the Hemi-powered E bodies of the year.

The J-code 429 Cobra Jet ram-air engine in any of the Torino bodies is a wonderful combination. According to the Marti Report, a total of 429,134 Ford Torinos were produced for the 1970 model year in all configurations and engine options. The Cobra was the top dog offering, with 7,675 customers choosing the high-performance package. Pricing was reasonable, in the $4,500 range—more than a less luxurious Road Runner and less than an LS6-equipped Chevelle SS454.

⬆ The Cobra package came in multiple varieties for 1970. If you looked low on the fender between the front wheel well and the door, you might catch a glimpse of this cubic inch callout.

⬆⬆ The Torino Cobra models shared the same instrument panel with the rest of Ford's intermediate-sized models.

Northwest Dealer Special

THE OREGON AND WASHINGTON Ford Dealers Association got together with an idea to promote the newly revamped 1970 Torino body style. Its members devised a special Torino two-door hardtop body style that would have a distinctive and sporty look aimed at the youthful buyer. Offered in a full range of V-8 options, including the big-block Cobra 429 CJ with its unique N/W graphics, the plan was to special order 600 units, but sales dictated that only 395 were made.

Available in three Grabber colors—Washington Green, Pacific Blue, and Oregon Orange—with a black hood, the package included dual racing mirrors, dual chrome hood-lock pins, rocker-panel stripes, and Argent-painted styled steel wheels.

The Kansas City District chose to run a similar promotion centered only on the Mach 1, Ranchero, and Cobra models. This promotion made an additional ninety "Twister" Cobra 429 CJ versions of the car, which mostly included the ram-air SCJ and Drag Pack options.

Overall Torino GT sales grew slightly for 1970, while the Cobra models dropped by about 50 percent from the 1969 totals. The J-code 429 CJ Cobra option (rated at 375 horse-power) would continue into the 1971 model year, although the Drag Pak rear gear ratios were dropped from the option list and never made it into production in the Torino Cobra body. All 1971 SCJ motors went into the Mustang or Cougar platform.

⬆ The Twister Special decal and promotion were shared with ninety-six 1970 Mustang Mach 1 models, all of which were painted in the Grabber Orange hue.

⬆ The 1970 Ford Cobra's factory shaker hood scoop was so named because the engine and hood scoop visibly shook with the uneven idle of the motor as the scoop protruded through the hood.

↑↑ There were ninety Ford Cobra Twister specials created by the Kansas City dealers as a special model to promote sales.

↑ In addition to the ninety Vermilion (Calypso Coral) Cobras made for the Kansas City District, there were another two Ford Rancheros identically equipped. Only one of the two Twister Rancheros has been discovered.

Ill-Fated: The King Cobra

FORD NEEDED a NASCAR body to go with the semihemi Boss 429 as the next progression of the Talladega of 1969½. Designed by Larry Shinoda, the new effort was based on the much sleeker profile of the 1970 Ford Torino and Mercury Montego fastback. Shinoda added a wedge-shaped nose cone, reshaped front fenders, and a hood that reduced drag. The design was expected to become the ultimate 200-mile-per-hour Ford.

But NASCAR was busy tinkering with the rules. In 1970 the league changed the homologation requirement from five hundred to three thousand cars. This meant that to qualify to race, a manufacturer had to build and sell three thousand vehicles or powerplants. Oddly, the powerplant was not required to be sold in the body seeking qualification. Ford's plan was to combine sales of the Boss 429 Mustang, for the engine, with sales of the King Cobra Torino and Montego Cyclone Spoiler II for body numbers to meet the rules.

The plan was not carried out. In September 1969 Bunkie Knudsen was fired as Ford president by Henry Ford II and replaced by his corporate rival, Lee Iacocca. Iacocca felt that both smaller cars and personal luxury cars were the next wave for vehicle sales, and NASCAR advanced neither segment. Iacocca would lead Ford for the next eight years, prioritizing the Pinto and the Mustang II in place of any new muscle-car development.

The King Cobra was slated to receive the top Boss 429, grossly underrated at 375 horsepower. All three King Cobras were equipped with a four-speed manual and Hurst shifter, 9-inch rear end with 3.50:1 gear ratio, power steering, and front disc brakes. Only seven examples were ordered to be built with this unique design. Of those seven only three were completed: two Torino King Cobras and one Mercury version labeled as the Cyclone Spoiler II. Two were built with the Boss 429, and one King Cobra was created with a 429 SCJ. They appeared to have been given by Ford to major NASCAR racing teams, such as Holman-Moody and others, with only three known to survive today. Sadly none of the three saw any competitive track time, although the good news is that all three are in collectors' hands.

➡ Shown here, Larry Shinoda is supervising the nearly completed 1970 Ford Torino King Cobra, one of three built. By the time the car would have appeared on NASCAR's ovals, the program was effectively outlawed by the sanctioning body. And when the 1970 Daytona 500 was run in February 1970, Shinoda, along with Ford president Bunkie Knudson, had already been fired by Henry Ford II, on September 11, 1969, not long after this photo of Shinoda and the development team was taken.

Mercury Cyclone Spoiler 429 SCJ

THE MERCURY COUNTERPART to the Torino Cobra was labeled the Cyclone Spoiler. It lived up to its name with prominent front and rear spoilers. Although the Ford Torino and Mercury Montego shared the same platform and assembly line, the Mercury designers were crafty in disguising the sleek lines of the Torino in an outrageous pointed nose design with a centered "gun-sight" grille that worked to successfully divide both the aerodynamics and those who either love or hate the frontal look of the car. The center extension created a deep recess on each side, which displayed the quad headlights.

A hidden headlight option added a sense of horizontal consistency across the unseemly grille. Unlike the multiple Ford two-door offerings of the Torino and Cobra, the high-performance Cyclone Spoiler was built only upon the semifastback body. Mercury did not offer the full fastback or the two-door post in the Montego line. The overall design of the Montego was right at 210 inches, as compared to the Torino's 206 inch length.

The Montego MX shared the same body as the Cyclone Spoiler but lacked the performance appearance. The MX was available with the N-code 429 rated at 360 horsepower. The 375-horsepower J-code 429 was not available on the MX. Both the C6 automatic and the four-speed transmission were available for the Montego performance packages. The 375-horsepower 429 required the Cyclone Spoiler option, which, like the Cobra, could be ordered with the Drag Pak option, converting the Cobra Jet

▲ The Mercury Cyclone package combined subtle performance with a Jimmy Durante–style front end. At the time the car was heavily criticized for its extended snout.

engine into a Super Cobra Jet package. One major difference was the absence of a shaker hood scoop on the J-code Ram-Air package. It was replaced by a very stealthy low-profile integrated hood scoop in the center of the expansive beaked hood. The Cyclone weighed in at a stout 3,816 pounds, 40 pounds bulkier than its Torino Cobra counterpart. Where Mercury bested the Cobra was in the unique four-gauge package, which included a large tachometer, oil pressure, amps, and water temperature monitors recessed into the dash to the right of the driver.

For 1970 Mercury sold a combined total of 120,000 Montegos and Cyclones, with fewer than 13,500 of those cars wearing the elusive Cyclone decal. These figures showed a marginal increase of 3.5 percent over Mercury's 1969 total production. By the end of the production year, Ford would sell more than four times as many Torinos as Mercury sold of their intermediate model. Mercury's one bragging point was a whopping 11 percent of all Montegos sold carried Cyclone or the Cyclone Spoiler moniker.

While the distinctive nose of the Mercury Montego attracted a lot of attention on the street, it also captured a lot of wind and proved to be less than aerodynamic during preseason testing. For this reason, the Mercury-sponsored racing teams stayed with the proven 1969-bodied extended-nose Cyclone Spoiler. The 1970 body design would not be raced competitively until 1972, when the Wood Brothers, with David Pearson at the wheel, campaigned the NASCAR circuit sponsored by Purolator.

◤ The Mercury Cyclone interior is short on gauges and pizzazz. When the Cyclone Spoiler option was included, the dash received four additional pods in the dash pad that housed instruments to monitor a performance motor. ⬆ The Mercury Cyclone shared the SportsRoof semifastback roofline of the Ford Torino. The six taillights set on an Argent panel are a strong contrast to Ford's single wall-to-wall taillight option.

IN 1970, with a second-year restyling up front that included a bolder grille treatment, the Eliminator package was featured in the 1970 Cougar dealer brochure where Mercury claimed:

↑ The biggest change for 1970, as seen on this small-block 1970 Cougar Eliminator 302, was the split front grille, which replaced 1969's full-width version.

COUGAR ELIMINATOR . . . SPOILERS HOLD IT DOWN . . . NOTHING HOLDS IT BACK Eliminator is a hardcore high performer and offers hardware to match. Front and rear spoilers are a clue, and so are the racing mirrors, the blackout grille, the tough hood, with its black scoop and stripe, the black wheels with hub caps and trim rings, the full-length Eliminator stripe. For proof positive there's a four-barrel 351 cubic inch V-8 under the hood (300-horsepower), a 3.25:1 rear axle, F70 × 14 belted traction tires, full competition suspension system with heavy-duty shocks and springs, and a rear stabilizer bar. The cockpit is completely in character: high-back bucket seats, a full spread of instruments and switches (including 6000 rpm tachometer, oil pressure gauge, rally clock with sweep second hand and E.T. indicator) set in a field of black, two-spoke steering wheel with pad-blow horn, and a visual panel housing door-ajar and low-fuel signal. You can further breed your Cougar Eliminator with any number of high-performance options, from Styled Steel Wheels to Drag Pak, from a 4-speed gearbox with Hurst Shifter® to the Detroit No-Spin Locker rear axle. V-8 engines? From Boss 302 to CJ 428-4V with Ram Air induction. Ask your Mercury dealer for a complimentary copy of his special high-performance catalog.

In 1970 Eliminator sales saw a meager uptick to 2,268 units, while Cougar sales declined 25 percent overall. Just 469 Boss 302s were produced, of which 1,424 had the standard 351-4V standard engine, while 374 428s (both CJ and SCJ variants) found their way behind the leaping cougar hood emblem.

Like other muscle cars in 1970, the Boss 302 saw an expanded options list. The optional Magnum 500 wheels got chrome plating. Dealers responded by ordering heavily optioned cars for their inventory. Gone were the limited color choices, and most 302s came with scoops, stripes, and spoilers.

In 2017 we had the opportunity to photograph three 1970 Eliminator Boss 302 Cougars for *Legendary Cougar* magazine, a publication devoted to the classic Cougar era (1967 to 1973). The cars provided several different variations on the Eliminator Boss 302 theme, all three in Competition Blue. For 1970, in-the-know Cougar enthusiasts consider the Eliminator Boss 302 to be at the pinnacle of the Mercury muscle-car hierarchy. The first characteristic to note is the model's exceptional balance, which had been refined over five years beginning with the 1967 model. The chassis received continual development, in part due to Mercury's Trans-Am racing program.

The Eliminator featured staggered rear shocks to keep its rear axle planted, while front and rear antisway bars, high-rate springs, and performance-calibrated shocks all around contributed to the Eliminator's exceptional road manners for the era. And there was the Boss 302 engine itself, a $388.60 option in 1970—even more expensive than the $310.90 428 Cobra Jet option. The Super Drag Pak option added the Detroit Locker rear, engine oil gauge, and 4.30:1 rear axle ratio, plus an extra $207.30 to the car's sticker price.

The polar opposite of the Boss 302 variant was the Eliminator equipped with either of the 428 engine options, Cobra Jet (CJ) or Super Cobra Jet (SCJ). These are the bruisers, designed to go head to head with its big-displacement, big-block pony-car competitors, the AMC Javelin 390, the Chevrolet Camaro Z/28, the Ford Mustang Boss 429, and the Pontiac Firebird Trans Am.

⬇ When the second-generation Cougars were introduced for the 1969 model year, they received 302- and 428-cubic-inch Eliminator models. This carried over to 1970 with styling updates.

The 428's genesis arose through the synthesis of several components from Ford's performance-parts bin. It first came together in 1967 at Tasca Ford, the performance-oriented dealership in Rhode Island.

Key pieces included a 428 Police Interceptor block, free-breathing cylinder heads from the 1963½ Galaxie 406, a stock 1967 390 GTA camshaft, the aluminum Police Interceptor intake, the same Holley four-barrel carb used on Ford's all-conquering Ford GT race cars, 3/8-inch fuel lines to a 427-type fuel pump, a 427 dual-point distributor, Fairlane-type exhaust headers feeding a 2¼-inch exhaust, plus other bits such as a Shelby GT350 power steering pulley and a 6-quart deep sump oil pan.

Period road tests show that a 428 SCJ with its advertised 335 horsepower (the same output was listed for ram-air and non-ram-air versions) would sprint from 0 to 60 in just 5.4 seconds and cover the quarter mile in 14.10 seconds with a speed across the finish-line marker of 103 miles per hour.

A deep examination of the production numbers shows that seven non-XR7 428 CJ Cougars were built in 1970, while the 428 CJ found its way into sixty-six of the more deluxe XR7 convertibles. A total of thirty-seven of those XR7s were equipped with the ram-air option, thirty-three with the C6 three-speed automatic and just four with the four-speed manual. One can imagine the torque flex when applying one's right foot to the accelerator pedal on a 428 CJ–equipped Eliminator convertible.

Based on its size, engine, and power-to-weight ratio, might this Cougar hardtop be the pinnacle for Mercury's muscle cars?

↑ In this very rare group photograph, three 1970 Mercury Cougar Eliminator 302s pose for *Legendary Cougar Magazine*. Only 323 Cougar Eliminators were produced for 1970. You're looking at 1 percent of that year's total production.

Buick, Oldsmobile, and Pontiac

Buick GSX

Oldsmobile 442 W-30 and W-31

Pontiac GTO Ram Air and 455

Pontiac Trans Am 400

Buick, Oldsmobile, and Pontiac (BOP) muscle cars are often grouped together, as the General Motors marketing team choose to internally segment these brands separate from Chevrolet and Cadillac. Although two of the three no longer exist—Oldsmobile and Pontiac were eliminated as part of GM's downsizing in the 2000s leading up to its bankruptcy—during the 1960s muscle-car era each division worked hard to create a market distinction from the others.

BUICK

Buick had established itself as the car for the white-collar worker who had "arrived" and could afford a little more luxury than a basic Chevrolet but didn't fit the stodgy image of a Cadillac owner. This allowed Buick just enough latitude to create a subtle performance package that attracted the mature owner looking for more than bucket seats and a floor shifter.

Buick introduced Grand Sport (GS) models in 1965. When their Riviera gained the GS emblems that year, it included the largest Buick engine at 425 cubic inches with dual carburetors, a distinct difference from the luxury image the average Riviera projected. This theme would continue until the ultimate high-performance Buick was released in 1970, the GSX model, advertised in a vibrant Saturn Yellow paint that demanded attention. Black stripes down the hood, along the sides, and across a raked rear spoiler defied Buick's country-club "gentleman's muscle car" image.

OLDSMOBILE

Oldsmobile was another brand trapped by the luxury image it had worked hard to establish. In fact Oldsmobile released its first postwar high-compression V-8 engine six years before Chevrolet. The division also was first to introduce tri-power carburetion on an American V-8 in 1957 on its J-2 model. By the late 1960s Oldsmobile was known as a more mature car for a driver demanding more refinement than could be found in the comparable Chevrolets and Pontiacs. (GM's well-crafted postwar brand hierarchy ran from affordable Chevrolet to Pontiac, Oldsmobile, Buick, and finally the most luxurious Cadillac.)

Based in Lansing, Michigan, Oldsmobile started the muscle-car wars alongside the Pontiac GTO in 1964 with the 442 option on the midsize Cutlass. The number 442 signified four-barrel carb, four-speed transmission, and dual exhausts. (There was even a four-door version of the 442 depicted in a first-year advertisement—shown driven by two police officers in an artist's conception featured in an ad in *Motor Trend* in spring 1964.) By the end of the 1960s, the 442 was a known muscle car and Oldsmobile's only real performance offering going into 1970.

PONTIAC

Pontiac created its model distinction in the late 1950s with the help of marketing marvel Jim Wangers, who worked at Pontiac's ad agency, Campbell Ewald. Wangers wanted to emphasize Pontiac's wide-body design, introduced in 1959. Pontiac marketing during this period illustrated the wide and low attributes needed for a well-handling road car in a land-mark series of ads and brochure images penned by illustrators Art Fitzpatrick and Van Kaufman. Wangers's brilliance was to have artist's conceptions of the car that adjusted the dimensions ever so slightly to create a lower, longer, wider appearance, when in fact the 1959 body shell was a shared platform across all GM models. His crafty marketing campaign helped Pontiac launch the 1964 GTO in bold style. Central to the effort's success was having ringer examples of the new model tuned by Ace Wilson's Royal Pontiac in Royal Oak, Michigan, and sent to the various magazines. The most legendary was the 1964 Pontiac Tempest GTO that appeared on the cover of the March 1964 issue of *Car and Driver* magazine, where it was compared to . . . a Ferrari 250 GTO. So much for truth in marketing!

Pontiac created a speed-focused image separate from its divisional rivals, especially Buick and Oldsmobile. Over the next forty-five years, until the brand was discontinued in GM's painful post-bankruptcy restructuring, Pontiac was recognized as GM's performance brand—especially in the 1960s, when it was helmed by the legendary John DeLorean, who would go on to build his own midengine sports car in the 1980s.

As priorities shifted toward more efficient, cleaner, safer cars, global players became fierce competitors for the American car buyer's dollar. But for a glorious period when a car's value was linked directly to what happened when the go pedal went flat, the Buick, Pontiac, and Oldsmobile teams developed unique performance niches, offering cars remembered and treasured decades after they rolled off their respective assembly lines.

FIFTY YEARS ON, it's getting more difficult to get an inside look into the development of what we now recognize as being the pinnacle of the muscle-car era, the cars of 1970. But more than a decade ago, we were privy to such a situation.

When talking about the muscle cars of 1970, one that is often overlooked is the Buick GSX. It was, and remains, one of the era's quintessential muscle cars.

It's common practice in the automobile industry for executives and engineers to evaluate development mules and early production vehicles, often called "fast-feedback" vehicles. Driving these vehicles home from work, often in camouflage, has long been a common occurrence in southern Michigan households and was certainly the case for Ron Frahm, now retired, who spent almost forty years at GM, mostly working refining the ride and handling in a number of Buicks. He was the lead engineer on the GSX.

Ron's son Dan, who today works for General Motors himself, located this GSX online, and he notes that one unique component on this model is its wheels. For the GSX, Buick had Motor Wheel develop a 15×7 wheel that was coded WG. This wheel had a specific offset—you can usually tell whether it's correct by seeing whether a quarter can sit on the lip without falling off. The wheels on this car were indeed WG, but they needed some attention to be perfect. Joe Gauzek, who worked on these

⬆ The 1970 GSX was Buick's big-block entry in the muscle car wars. Often referred to as a gentleman's hot rod, it was available with two versions of Buick's 455-cubic-inch V-8. A standard version produced 350 horsepower at 4,600 rpm, and this Stage 1 version produced an advertised 360 (underrated) horsepower, also at 4,600 rpm.

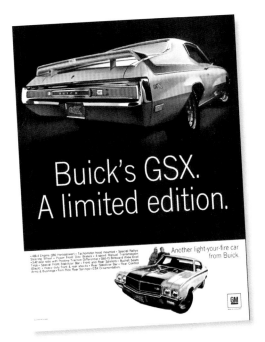

Buick's GSX.
A limited edition.

Another light-your-fire car from Buick.

↑ Buick let the pictures do the talking with this 1970 GSX introductory advertisement that listed the package components without any of the usual creative salesmanship.

↓ The Buick GSX was based on the same midsize, full-frame chassis as the GTO and SS Chevelle. Buick threw out its usual sophisticated subtlety when the GSX package was released in Saturn Yellow with bold black horizontal stripes outlined in Blood Red.

wheels originally at Motor Wheel, helped with the restoration to original specs. The center disc of the wheel was cut away from the rim to get the rim surfaced and chromed. The center discs were originally bright chromed, then glass-bead blasted to keep the chrome from cracking under the stress. The chrome was fine. The wheels just needed repainting of the flat black paint on the centers for a perfect restoration.

In the world of GM muscle cars, the GSX is a relatively rare find. Just 678 were built in 1970 (about half of the projected volume), and it was available in just two colors: Saturn Yellow (491) and Apollo White (187). Out of the 678 cars, 199 had four-speed manual transmissions, 479 were equipped with the optional three-speed automatic. A total of 278 had standard 455 engines with 350 horsepower, while the other 400 were Stage 1–powered with 360 horsepower, costing an additional $115 (both had 510 foot-pounds torque, and these numbers were very understated for the benefit of the insurance companies). In 1970, the GSX package cost $1,195 and included much more than the special stripes.

In a 2008 interview, Ron Frakes gave the author some insights into the GSX's development. He started with GM in the experimental engineering department at the GM Proving Grounds in Milford, Michigan. From Milford, Ron moved to Buick Motor Division, where he worked in reliability, then to product engineering as a test engineer, design engineer, and finally development engineer. Much of his effort was directed toward designing Buick to be acoustically quiet and developing the ride and handling along with body and frame structure and road isolation.

Ron noted that in the mid- and late 1960s Buick had some fairly hot Skylark GS models but did not have a designated muscle-car name like the Olds 442 or the Pontiac GTO. Buick management decided it needed a standout car that would compete with its sister divisions. That car would become the GSX.

Frakes explained that one major problem with the GSX release was that much of the content of the vehicle was changing until nearly the start of production. That included such things as the specific steering wheel, the GSX instrument-panel emblem, the hood tach, and, most importantly, the front spoiler.

This last was Frakes's responsibility, and his initial design had it attached directly to the bottom flange of the front bumper, which was very effective. However, it quickly became apparent that it would be unable to clear many driveway inclines. Something had to change. He redesigned the spoiler and moved it rearward, nearer to the front tires, to provide for an adequate ramp angle. This move effectively changed the spoiler to an air dam that pushed air up through the radiator and eliminated any downforce on the front. The last step was to add the flat polypropylene panel between the bottom of the front bumper and the top of the spoiler. This solved the problem and re-created the front downforce required.

The car's development continued to evolve as the first production-spec GSX models were produced. Frakes's team discovered that the rear spoilers were cracking along the joint between the upper and lower halves as they progressed through the paint ovens. They quickly increased the width of the joint to ½-inch minimum and created a vent in the center underneath side to provide pressure relief.

But the biggest threat, as Frakes noted in his original 2008 interview, was that several months before the GSX introduction, the insurance companies changed the insurance cost structure. Now, the higher the horsepower-to-weight ratio of a vehicle, the higher the insurance premiums. This, in Frakes's opinion, effectively killed the muscle-car era. The effect on the GSX was to essentially cut the projected volume in half for the 1970 model year with no follow-up for 1971.

The Buick GSX represents a special era in GM history. It was a time when a small team of engineers were empowered to produce cars with lasting—dare we say legendary—appeal, hardly restrained in their zeal to surpass the efforts of their colleagues in other GM divisions as well as their Motor City competitors. For Buick, the GSX stands tall, clearly illustrating that the "gentleman's muscle car" left a legacy that stands among Flint's finest.

◀ Most muscle cars in 1970 carried a more aggressive look at the front. Buick achieved this with twin hood scoops buried in the top of the hood, twin jet black hood and trunk stripes, body-color headlight surrounds, and a lower flat black air dam. A hood-mounted tachometer pod is hidden in the Gloss Black area of the hood.

▲ The twin functional hood scoops force-feed air to the 455-cubic-inch Buick V-8 engine. Stage 1 designated the most powerful V-8 Buick offered in the muscle car era. Buick developed an additional Stage 2 package for over-the-counter sales in order to prep a car for race-only tune.

⬆ This side-profile view shows this 1970 Oldsmobile Cutlass' near-perfect proportions. Black paint and gold accent stripes really suit this car.

THE GLOVES WERE FINALLY OFF in 1970: GM lifted the 400-cubic-inch ceiling for this year's intermediate models. Oldsmobile would no longer need to hide behind paperwork when replacing the 400-cubic-inch engine with a 455, as if Hurst, which never handled the engine conversion, had swapped out the motors for 1968 and '69 H/O cars.

Not only could Oldsmobile engineers include the 455 in the 442 offerings, but they could also finally unleash one of the "Hot Ones" that had been kicking around behind the secretive walls hiding the GM test track. The W numbers identified Oldsmobile's drivetrain and engine options in the way Chevrolet used the L prefix. The public had been aware of the W-30 package, with its tongue-in-cheek increase of only 10 horsepower over the standard offering, since 1966. This 10-horsepower gain involved a larger cam, different heads, and a factory ram-air system to gulp air from below the front bumper. The W-31 option signified the high-winding, lightweight small-block power that appeared in 1968 under the Ram-Rod marketing label and featured the crossed-piston front fender decal. Now that same group of designers from Lansing was bringing out the big guns with all 370 horsepower. It seems a little funny that the Olds engineers would put all this work into a special W-30 455 engine and be satisfied with a measly gain of 5 horsepower over the standard 455-cubic-inch offering. Do you think maybe they were less than completely honest with their slide rules?

Perception did not always correspond directly with reality when it came to advertised horsepower in 1970. The insurance companies were now decoding the new car VINs hoping to determine the risk they engaged when underwriting these performance cars; then manufacturers started seeing the negative results of this in the showroom, with many young buyers unable to take delivery of their high-performance cars due to the weighty insurance costs stacking up on top of the car payment. To give their buyers a little help, the manufacturers and marketing teams in got conservative with horsepower ratings in the sales literature. A more realistic estimate for the output from the W-30 package with the four-speed manual transmission would be 440 horsepower. The transmission choice mattered, as Oldsmobile inserted a different and more aggressive camshaft in the engines destined for manual transmission versus automatic.

It wasn't just about the horsepower, either. Torque won races, and both Buick and Oldsmobile knew how to test the mettle of a drivetrain with the torque created to launch the car forward from a dead stop. Oldsmobile did not shy away from these numbers and accurately declared the 500 foot-pounds of torque created by the W-30 package.

The W-30 option used the same basic block as all other 455 Oldsmobiles in 1970. The extra grunt was in the pistons, compression ratio, heads, and cam. The standard 455 offered a reasonable 9.5:1 compression ratio. The W-30 label meant ultra-high compression at a solid 10.5:1, requiring premium fuel. The manual-transmission W-30 motor came with a 328-degree cam with plenty of overlap and a special Quadrajet carburetor without primary metering rods—suspiciously rated at the same 370 horsepower as the automatic-transmission W-30 with the tamer 285/287-degree cam identical to the non–W-30 package 442 engine.

Both versions of the engine came with special-casting F-code heads. Designed for better air movement, these heads are highly sought after and can command more money today as loose cores than a W-30 442 cost new in 1970. The package also included an aluminum intake manifold and a special distributor. To verify the original motor in the 442, the engine is stamped on the driver's side of the block below the cylinder head with the engine and transmission combination plus the serial number of the car in which it was originally installed. Verifying these numbers is essential to determining the origin of a 442 and making certain it started life as a W-30 package car. The only two stamped codes that determine the W-30 are TS for the 370-horsepower with manual, and TT for the 370-horsepower with automatic.

Not only was the engine a fresh design for 1970, but so was the Cutlass exterior. Although the A-body Oldsmobile remained a full-frame platform and retained the basic shape and dimensions from the previous redesign in 1968, both the front fenders and the quarters received a style line that gave the impression of bulging muscles

⬇ The license plate says "1BADW30," which leaves no doubt as to what lurks under the twin-scooped hood.

hidden under a jacket. A wider and taller grille opening enhanced the muscular appearance, as did the W-25 dual snorkel ram-air hood. There was nothing subtle about the two broad scoops large enough to swallow a small child that flanked the hood centerline from the leading edge back. Oldsmobile even created a mad scientist character they referred to as "Doctor Olds" for the advertising campaign. One such ad identifies the engine as an "Elephant" engine in an attempt to lay claim on the term commonly associated to the Mopar 426 Hemi.

All W-30 Oldsmobiles had a few other distinctive features that help authenticate them besides the specific F-code heads and the specific part number Quadrajet carb. All came with red plastic front inner-wheel well liners, the afore mentioned W-25 dual snorkel ram-air hood with built-in twist-lock hood pins, a side body stripe that radiused over each wheel well, and a three-dimensional W-30 designation on each front fender behind the wheel opening. The rear bumper was designed with two reliefs to make way for the dual trumpet exhaust tips. Each wheel well also received wheel-lip moldings.

The W-30 package mandated a heavy-duty transmission—either the three-speed Turbo Hydramatic 400 or the close-ratio M21 four-speed manual with a positive-feel Hurst handle. The automatic could be column mounted or floor mounted if you specified the bucket seats and console options. Tilt wheel was available, as was a four-spoke custom sport steering wheel.

Interior choices for the Oldsmobile were never described as utilitarian. All the seating options were plush and comfortable with multiple details and a variety of colors, as was typical of General Motors in that era. There were six different color choices for the bucket seats, including cloth seat colors offered in either blue or gold. The dash included chrome rings around three circular pods. Most buyers chose to upgrade from the standard bench, but many combinations were possible, and some of the rarest W-30 cars ordered were the ones ordered with the fewest options.

For those who wanted a few creature comforts, Oldsmobile was happy to oblige. In addition to a choice of manual or automatic transmission, there was also the option of the Hurst console-mounted dual-gate shifter as seen in previous years on the Hurst Oldsmobile package.

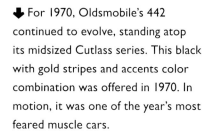

⬇ For 1970, Oldsmobile's 442 continued to evolve, standing atop its midsized Cutlass series. This black with gold stripes and accents color combination was offered in 1970. In motion, it was one of the year's most feared muscle cars.

Oldsmobile was the only GM division to offer a unique aluminum axle carrier under the W-27 code for the twelve-bolt corporate rear end. To dress up the 442, there were two versions of the Super Stock wheels: one was body color, and the other was detailed chrome. Dimensions remained 14×7 on all wheel choices. Rallye gauges, which included a tachometer, were a common choice, as was the rear deck wing spoiler.

With the 400-cubic-inch corporate limit for all GM intermediates gone in 1970, there was no Hurst and Oldsmobile collaboration even though Hurst proposed a Bright Yellow 1970 package. Oldsmobile management chose to pass and released its own small-block version, the Rallye 350 package.

The GM A-bodies retained their full-frame design even though most Ford, Dodge, Plymouth, and AMC counterparts had moved to unibody (unitized) construction for their midsize offerings. Even the F-body Camaro and Firebird had shed unwanted pounds by using a front subframe design. The advantage to the full frame was in managing the torque coming from the engines that Oldsmobile was now fitting in the intermediates. The W-30 package included the Rallye-sports suspension (F41) with front and rear heavy-duty springs, both sway bars, boxed lower rear control arms, 14×7 steel wheels with G70-14 white-letter Wide Oval tires. The standard W-30 rear gears were 3.42:1 for both automatic and manual. Interestingly the standard brakes were nonpower four-wheel drums, which the smart buyer would upgrade to the optional power front disc arrangement.

Exterior colors varied from mild to wild, with most Oldsmobiles appearing in more subdued hues, as the primary purchaser in 1970 may not have been your father but was generally old enough to be someone's father. The Cutlass 442 package was offered in three body styles. First was the two-door sedan (post) Sports Coupe, the lowest-cost version with the advantage of being stiffer in comparison to the pillarless two-door hardtop. Next was the Holiday coupe, which was a true two-door hardtop and the most popular choice. Third was a convertible.

Although the W-30 package was available on any of the three models, few buyers chose it with the Sports Coupe or the convertible, with 262 and 264 made, respectively. The majority of W-30 production went with the most traditional two-door hardtop, the Holiday coupe, with 2,574 units, or nearly 80 percent of the 3,100 W-30 442s made. With total 442 production tallying 22,877 units, the W-30 option was found on 13 percent of cars built—approximately one in eight 442s produced in 1970.

The little W-30 emblem was only located below the larger 442 callouts on each front fender. It was easy to overlook the first time you were challenged at the stoplight, but on no later encounter.

Although any 1970 442 was a force to be taken seriously, when it was equipped with an optional W-25 hood scoop, most thought twice about challenging the driver to a street race. When they also noticed that subtle W-30 emblem, they usually figured it was best to just go home and save certain embarrassment. When new and with the standard G70 bias-ply Wide Oval tires, *Car Craft* magazine was able to tune the W-30 to a sub-14-second quarter mile of 13.88 at 95.84 miles per hour. If the car had the rear gears replaced with more drag-strip-oriented numbers, it was capable of mid-13-second quarter-mile times through stock exhaust while listening to the Beach Boys on the optional factory-installed underdash stereo eight-track player.

⬆⬆ If you want to see how a dealer would deliver a brand new 1970 Oldsmobile 442, this reference-quality restoration is it. It's factory correct right down to the hang tags on the directional stalk and the rearview mirror.

⬆ The fender badging leaves no doubt as to what's under the hood.

⬆ This is the two-door sedan Cutlass S version of the W-31 package. It carried an MSRP of just $3,155 and could cover a quarter mile in just 14.92 seconds at 96.05 miles per hour according to a test published by *Hot Rod* magazine.

For its first year in 1968, the high-revving 350-cubic-inch small-block was marketed as the Ram Rod 350. The Ram Rod name did not excite buyers, however, and it sold only 732 units. For 1969 Olds changed the designation to W-31, to slightly better results at 913 copies made. By 1970 Oldsmobile was including it with the Big Block W-30 option in advertisements that called them the "W machines."

Like Chevrolet's LT1 small-block, the W-31 was built to make high horsepower from a limited displacement. It was an Oldsmobile 350-cubic-engine engine rated at 325 horsepower, but those with a good sense of power believed that Oldsmobile under-reported the number by more than 30 horsepower. The design included an aluminum intake manifold with a W-350 casting embossed in front of the large Rochester four-barrel carburetor. An aggressive camshaft and valvetrain kept up the high RPMs.

Running a camshaft crafted for high RPMs, the W-31's rough idle did not create enough vacuum for a power-brake booster to function. Therefore, a true W-31 will have manual brakes as well as a manual four-speed transmission with Hurst shifter. As with most high-performance option packages, air-conditioning was not available for the W-31. While most other Cutlass and 442 options could be added to the W-31, performance customers tended to go with the bare necessities.

The small-block W machine saw its final and most recognizable year in 1970. At first glance the W-25 ram-air hood might suggest a 442. With a little more inspection, the smallish W-31 emblem is visible on front fenders that share the 442 striping. The horsepower recipe would remain the same as the previous two years, with the oversize harmonic balancer and cylinder heads with a "6" casting number. The W-31 was available only in the Sports Coupe two-door sedan or the Holiday coupe. After three years of production the W-31 would not continue into 1971. Of the almost 3,000 units produced over three years, almost one-half were made in 1970, with 1,352 total units produced that year.

↓ This is a unique view of the Oldsmobile W-31 ram air cleaner with the vacuum actuated flapper valve. Under normal driving conditions, the valve remains closed, drawing the warmer engine air. When hard acceleration occurs, engine vacuum drops, releasing the spring-loaded valve and rerouting the cooler outside air through the hood scoop and into the engine for increased performance.

↑ The 1970 Oldsmobile with the W-31 package was offered only on the Cutlass product line and not the 442 package.

↑ Many muscle cars received red-line tires in the late 1960s, like this 1969 442. By the 1970 model year, the trend switched to white letter tires on performance models.

⬆ With the Pacific Ocean in the background, this 455-equipped two-door hardtop 1970 Pontiac GTO shows off its classic lines. Pontiac also offered a convertible for 1970, but just 3,615 were sold. This compares to 32,737 hardtops, including 3,629 Judges.

THE GTO RECEIVED A REFRESH for 1970. Gone were the hidden-headlight option as the four round headlamps were integrated into their own pods within the urethane nose. The front end retained the traditional Pontiac look of the pointed and split-center grille openings. The third year of this body style received a sheetmetal refresh, and the GTO returned in the fall with the addition of curves that hadn't been so obvious the year before. Above each wheel well was a new rounded accent that blended back into each door. When viewed from the full side of the GTO, this new architectural detail was commonly referred to as eyebrows. Gone, too, was the chrome front grille; now each front fender had a distinctive top edge that blended into the wide monochrome front nose piece. A touch of chrome remained with the integrated rear bumper, which now included larger taillights that wrapped around the rear corners to meet the required side marker lights. The bumper, called Endura, had the color pigment all the way through so any imperfections would not show.

The top-of-the-line GTO was "The Judge" package that continued into 1970. Although it was no longer available in the familiar Carousel Red color, the Judge package was now offered as an over-the-top addition to the existing GTO colors and included multicolored "eyebrow" decal accents independently applied above each wheel well. The trunk included an oversized wing that measured 60 inches wide and helped differentiate the GTO from GM's other A-body products. The Judge option added $332 to the price of a standard GTO and was available in either hardtop or convertible. In 1969 it had been the only GTO to receive the rear spoiler; for 1970 the spoiler was an available option on any GTO.

The Judge package also included two colorful front fender *The Judge* decals and a matching one on the trunk lid. The color combinations with the Judge option could be rather wild, with red and orange stripes available on a light Mint Turquoise paint. The Judge accents were available in three color motifs—orange, yellow, and black—creating some very striking visuals. The most notable color was a bright orange-yellow hue called Orbit Orange, which was the new feature color for the 1970 Judge but was also available on any GTO. What is interesting is when most other car models had incorporated sleek, body-colored, sport-style rearview mirrors, Pontiac still included the standard flimsy chrome mirror that looked more at home on the door of a mid-1960s Chevy II (Nova).

The interior received minor improvements as well, with more GTOs equipped with bucket seats and consoles, factory air-conditioning, and additional creature comforts. The dash now had an optional gauge package with an integrated tachometer, although many still chose the hood tachometer that had become a GTO trademark over the years. One of the most notable interior options added for 1970 was the flat Formula three-spoke steering wheel, replacing the more traditional three-spoke deep-set design. All cars equipped with the Ram Air received the Ram Air knob mounted under the dash above the brake pedal.

The handling was upgraded with the installation of a rear anti-roll bar, essentially the same bar as used on other GM high performance offerings. In order to further reduce body roll on corners, the front anti-roll bar was beefier as well. This was combined with a variable-ratio power steering system that reduced the turning radius. The end results of these hidden upgrades made the 1970 model a more enjoyable road car when said road included winding turns.

← From the rear, the 1970 GTO shared similar clean lines shared with other GM intermediates.

↑ As with many other 1970s muscle car makers, Pontiac offered a hood-mounted tach for the GTO.

↑↑ This Pontiac GTO is equipped with a four-speed manual gearbox. The engine turned trim on the dash offers a pop in an interior expanse of black vinyl.

An interesting option for the GTO that was both introduced and quickly canceled during the 1970 model year was a vacuum-operated exhaust (VOE) cutout feature. The VOE was activated by a pull-out knob to the left of the steering wheel, creating a loud open exhaust sound. Although this was available as an aftermarket component at the time, no new-car manufacturer had included it on the option list before. With new more restrictive state noise laws as well as safety issues with the exhaust exiting under the passenger compartment, however, the gutsy option was quickly canceled by GM management—but not before it had been equipped on 233 GTOs. All were restricted to the base-model 400-cubic-inch engine rated at 350 horsepower as opposed to any Ram Air or 455-cubic-inch cars.

There were three engine options for the 1970 Judge. The 455 engine was added for 1970 in the standard GTO but was held back until midyear for the Judge package. The 455 used the Ram Air III cam and was rated lower than the two 400-cubic-inch Ram Air versions at 360 horsepower. Those who read the full specs knew the increase in cubic inches benefited the engine with an increase of 500 foot-pounds of torque. The same engine installed in the Pontiac Grand Prix was rated at 370 horsepower. In order to eliminate (or add to) the confusion Pontiac choose to list the 455 at 366 horsepower for the GTO. The camshafts used in the GTO 455 HO were the same as the Ram Air III with slightly different specifications between the manual and automatic transmission versions.

The Ram Air III became the standard engine for the Judge Package. As in previous years, it had operational hood scoops sealed against the air cleaner for a true shot of cold outside oxygen to the 400-cubic-inch engine. It featured "D" exhaust ports, free-flowing exhaust manifolds, and a cast-iron intake manifold. Also like previous years, the Ram Air III used different camshafts based on the transmission that it was mated to, even though the horsepower rating did not falter. This was an optional engine for the standard GTO. Possibly as an oversight, the Ram Air III engine could be ordered with the standard floor-mounted and Hurst-shifted three-speed transmission. Twenty-one buyers either choose this configuration or overlooked making a choice for the four-speed on the order blank.

The Ram Air IV was a carryover option from 1969 with a slight bump in horsepower to 370. Transmission options were either the M20 wide-ratio manual or the TH400 three-speed automatic, both of which used floor-mounted Hurst shifters unless the car was ordered with bench seat and automatic transmission. Both the Ram Air III and IV engines had a stronger bottom end than most 400-cubic-inch Pontiac motors due to the addition of four-bolt mains, improved breathing through larger valves, better-designed heads, and an aluminum intake manifold holding a Rochester four-barrel carburetor. Atop all of this sat an open dual-scoop air cleaner with a 3-inch-tall foam seal on top making sure all the air made its way into the engine. All Ram Air cars had black-painted functional hood scoops in contrast to the body-colored hood.

As in previous years air-conditioning was optional, and it was ordered at a surprisingly high rate for a muscle car. While the Rallye II wheels were a common option on GTOs, the Judges did not include trim rings. The tires were a newly released Firestone GoodyearWide Oval 14-inch option. The chrome exhaust splitters were now stock-mounted out back through the cutout relief in the rear valance instead of the lower rear quarter panels in previous years. Posi-TractionSafe-T-Track limited-slip differential remained an option, with the most common rear gear ratio of 3.55 and optional gearing of 3.23, 3.73, or 3.90.

The three engine choices each brought its own advantages. The Ram Air III was the second-most powerful choice and was standard with the Judge package. It had a milder cam and was more "streetable" than the Ram Air IV with its high-lift cam. The 455 HO gave you equal performance to the Ram Air III on paper, but much more performance on the street due to the greater torque. The Ram Air IV had the most horsepower and the highest rpm capabilities. Which one was the fastest combination for 1970?

Although the 455 GTO had the more pedestrian rear gears, it performed almost one full second slower on the quarter mile than the Ram Air versions. It is still believed today that the Ram Air IV was the most powerful engine offered on the GTO in 1970 and in fact over the course of the first-generation GTO, from 1964 to 1972.

Even with the new facelift and bright psychedelic colors, the GTO would attain only enough sales to make it the third-strongest muscle car for 1970. It trailed behind its A-body cousin, the Chevelle SS, and the Plymouth Road Runner. The declining sales were directly hampered by the insurance companies' surcharges targeted at the young male driver, who may have had a lower car payment than insurance payments on a high-profile model. Sales were limited to 40,149 GTOs, down from over 70,000 the previous year and with fewer than 10 percent of those (3,797) optioned as the Judge. Only 168 Judge convertibles were ordered, as there were additional insurance premiums for all high-performance drop-top models due to a perception that convertibles were more dangerous in rollover accidents.

As far as rarity, the Judge convertible has the lowest production figures. The general consensus is that 6 of the 168 built were ordered with the 455 HO rated at 360 horsepower, which was a no-cost option. This leaves a count of 162 Ram Air III and Ram Air IV Judge convertibles made. For 1970 there were thirty-seven Ram Air IV GTO convertibles, of which twenty-four were four-speed manuals and thirteen were automatics; of the latter thirteen, only six were also ordered with the Judge option.

The year 1971 would see a continuation of the GTO but with reduced compression and performance. Included in that statement is the 1971 455 HO, which was dropped down to 335 horsepower due to a reduced 8.4:1 compression ratio. Only 10,532 GTOs were made in 1971 due to the outlandish insurance costs by then attached to the "first" muscle car. The 1971 455 HO was installed in one last year Judge package as a Judge 357 Judges in 1971 were so equipped, with 17 of those being convertibles.

Between the ever-increasing insurance costs and the decreasing compression ratios due to restrictive emission standards, the true American muscle car would peak in sales during 1969 and in horsepower during the 1970 model year, signifying that the best was a direct correlation to the death of the era.

⬆ Like other GM cars for 1970, Pontiac offered an underdash eight-track that could be fully integrated into the optional AM/FM four-speaker stereo.

⬆⬆ With its air cleaner removed, this 1970 Pontiac GTO is powered by Pontiac's fabled 455-cubic-inch V-8, exposing the four-barrel Rochester carburetor.

Pontiac Trans Am 400

⬆ The midyear introduction of the 1970 Pontiac Firebirds limited production to 3,196 units for the Trans Am model in the strike-shortened year. For 1970 only two colors were offered, white or blue with contrasting stripes. The base MSRP for the abbreviated 1970 model year was $4,305.

THE TRANS AM FIREBIRD WAS INTRODUCED midyear 1969 with a plan to compete in the Trans-Am racing series. One-half of the plan was for Pontiac to create a 303-cubic-inch high-performance V-8 to rival the Z/28 Camaro's 302-cubic-inch mill. When the new small-block engine got scuttled, Trans Am became an option package to improve the Firebird's performance image with an appearance that resembled the 1965–1966 Shelby Mustang. Pontiac succeeded in garnering the attention of the automotive press and selling a few cars (697) in the process.

Both Pontiac and Chevrolet planned for a major revamp of the shared F-body platform for 1970. Pontiac designer Bill Porter's goal for the new Firebird design was a lower, slightly wider, and longer look, giving a European flair. In previews the public supported the dramatic change in shape and curves, but the public would have to wait. The larger rear quarter sections proved difficult to form, requiring the factory tooling to be changed to a multistep stamping process that delayed production until February of 1970. The delay was further complicated by a union strike that negatively impacted GM's overall production capabilities.

When the Firebird was finally released to the public, the Trans Am package was not an afterthought but an integral part of Pontiac's plan for success. Colors were Polar White and Lucerne Blue with opposite-color hood, roof, and trunk stripe surrounded by an edge border. The hood stripe finished at a "baby" bird decal located on top of the front body-colored urethane nose. The Trans Am phoenix would continue to grow over the next decade until it covered the majority of the hood.

A Trans Am without any additional options had a base price of $4,305, a hefty $750 more than the 1969 TA package. A well-equipped Trans Am could easily break the $5,000 threshold, pushing the cost into Corvette territory. The new "soft" nose was a larger application of the GTO urethane nose introduced in 1968. The body-colored monochrome front look contributed to the new European image that Pontiac was hoping to achieve with the second-generation Firebird.

This Trans Am was factory-equipped with the 335-horsepower Ram Air III engine with either the M20 four-speed manual or M40 Turbo HydraMatic 400 automatic transmission and a twelve-bolt 3.55 Safe-T-Track rear end. Most were also ordered with factory console and armrest. One complaint about the tall Hurst shifter installed with the console was the long throw when reaching for third gear. A little more bend in the shifter arm would have created a more ergonomic environment.

The two exterior colors were offered with three color choices for the interior. Blue appears to have been the most common, but black and white were also available. The distinction between a normal second-gen Firebird and the Trans Am package was displayed from all angles. Besides the distinctive color combinations, each Trans Am came with the shaker hood scoop, which—unlike Ford's versions—faced rearward. This design worked similarly to the Chevelle SS rear-facing cowl, which gathered air deflected off the windshield. Additionally each Trans Am received a three-piece spoiler across the front of the car and extending in front of the wheels. Two functional vents located high and to the rear of each front fender moved air out of the engine compartment. Out back the Trans Am included two more flares ahead of the rear tires and a three piece "ducktail" spoiler that framed the taillight panel. At highway speeds, the aerodynamic additions created 50 pounds of downforce, assisting in the superb handling characteristics.

The car sat low with a very stylized rear window area that created a rounded fastback shape. Although appealing from the outside, the sloping rear glass limited seating practicality for tall back-seat passengers. And despite the 108-inch wheelbase, legroom was also stingy in the rear—making the car, in keeping with its European design aspirations, a true 2+2. Each rear seat cushion was recessed, with the carpeted driveshaft tunnel dividing the two rear passengers. Because the new rounded body design did not translate well into a convertible offering, none were factory-produced in the second-generation F-body.

The interior had a cockpit feel with two large round gauges and five small round gauges overlaid with a turned aluminum dash face under a heavily padded top behind a three-spoke Formula steering wheel. The seating position was low, bringing the top of the door higher relative to the driver's shoulder than in previous years. Sitting low, as in a sports car, promoted the sense of improved handling. All Trans Ams were equipped with a quick 12.1:1 variable-ratio power steering and standard 10.9-inch power front disc brakes with 9.5-inch rear drums.

The lower center of gravity assisted in the handling department and remained a key characteristic of the new Trans Am. The front suspension comprised upper and lower control arms, heavy-duty coil springs, and a stout 1.25-inch front stabilizer bar that succeeded in keeping the car flat on twisty roads. In the rear, the leaf-spring suspension included heavy-duty shocks and a large (⅞-inch) stabilizer bar keeping the 15×7 inch Rallye II wheels squarely on the ground. In order to create the 15-inch version of the Rallye II wheels, Pontiac used the existing 14-inch wheel centers with a 15×7 outer rim. Shod in P245/60R15 BFGoodrich radial T/As, large for the period, the car's road manners did not disappoint.

⬆ The all-vinyl, bucket seat interior found on the second-generation Pontiac Firebird Trans Am was a comfortable environment. This example is equipped with the center console through which the four-speed shifter emerges.

⬆⬆ BFGoodrich radial T/A tires were not available back in 1970. Coming from the factory, the tire fitment was G70×14 Firestone Wide Ovals with the popular Rally II wheels.

Of the 49,000 Firebirds produced between Norwood, Ohio, and Van Nuys, California, only 3,196 were Trans Ams, which were built in the shortened 1970 production year. Of those, approximately one-third (1,084) were ordered in the optional Lucerne Blue. Unlike a lot of the other top packaged cars offered in 1969 and 1970, you could order your Trans Am with an automatic transmission and air-conditioning—in fact, almost one-third (988) of Trans Ams had air-conditioning, and one in four included both options. Still, more than half of buyers went for the four-speed, making 1,769 cars so equipped—another similarity to European preferences.

Each Trans Am came standard with the Pontiac 400-cubic-inch Ram Air III, rated at 345 horsepower with a strong 430 foot-pounds of torque. The new high-flow heads with 2.11/1.77-inch valves and large 72cc combustion chambers created a compression ratio of 10.5:1. Shifting was offered with the wide-ratio Muncie M20 or close-ratio M21 four-speed manual. The Turbo 400 three-speed automatic was also available.

The optional Ram Air IV increased the horsepower to 370, which was brought to the ground through either the M20 wide-ratio manual or the TH400 three-speed automatic. The engine produced the 25-horsepower increase with an additional 15 foot-pounds of torque. Only eighty-eight Trans Ams were equipped with the Ram Air IV—twenty-four from Van Nuys and the other sixty-four from Norwood. The Ram Air III and IV engines both included a stronger bottom end via four bolt mains, improved heads, and matching Rochester four-barrel carburetor mounted on an aluminum intake manifold.

Critics received the new Firebird favorably. The lower center of gravity made up for the increased girth and 3,650-pound weight. Improved handling raised the Firebird and Trans Am from the pony-car category into the sports-car market and allowed Pontiac to charge more for a superior product. The 57 percent front weight bias was typical for an American muscle car, but the great handling allowed one to manage braking nosedives and bring the tail around corners with a little right-foot steering. Although the car shined in the curves, its muscle-car credentials were tested on the straight track. The TA package with Ram Air IV would break into the high 13 seconds with speeds over 102 miles per hour. Muscle-car territory and the ability to take a corner—what a great combination. So good, in fact, that variations of the Trans Am second generation would continue for another twelve years.

↑ The United Auto Workers (UAW) strike against GM delayed the introduction of the second-generation Pontiac Firebird. The engine for the Trans Am version was Pontiac's 400-cubic-inch V-8, which produced either 345 horsepower for the Ram Air III or 370 horsepower for the optional Ram Air IV version.

❧ The clean styling of the second-generation Pontiac Trans Am is apparent from this angle. The early cars featured a smaller rear backlight (back window). Starting with the 1974 model year, Firebirds and Camaros received a wrap-around backlight.

Two Scoops: The Formula 400

DESIGNER BILL PORTER didn't actually like the shaker scoop design as introduced on the Trans Am. His approach was to keep all of the contours round with soft edges to enhance the low, sleek architecture of the new platform. For this reason he wanted a pair of air scoops reaching forward at the front edge of the hood to grab the airflow as it was disturbed by the nose. But design chief Bill Mitchell over-ruled Porter, feeling that a more muscular approach would set the Trans Am aside from the other F-body offerings. Porter's distinctive twin-scoop hood did make the Firebird family, however, appearing on both the Formula 350 and 400 models.

To save some pain on the purchase price and insurance cost of the new Trans Am, the savvy buyer could order the Firebird Formula 400 with the same Ram Air III engine and drivetrain. The Formula package included the dual snor-kel Ram Air hood, F41 suspension package, 12.1:1 power steering, and power front disc brakes with heavy-duty 9.5-inch rear drums. It was not quite the Trans Am package, but it would produce the same straightline performance if it was identically outfitted and would save the buyer 10 percent on the window sticker and close to 30 percent on the insurance costs. For this savings there was a reduction in street cred due to the missing front and rear spoilers, fender vents, over-the-top stripes, and shaker scoop. The Formula 400 package weighed about 100 pounds less than the Trans Am and was actually the preferred setup for those seeking the lowest quarter-mile elapsed times. A hundred pounds svelter meant $\frac{1}{10}$ of a second quicker in the quarter mile versus the Trans Am. The Formula 350 and 400 offerings were known as strong performers in their own right.

3. The Firebird Formula 400.

Formula 400 is a special breed of road car. What makes it special is the genuine practicality of its design . . . the appropriateness of its equipment . . . and the totality with which it performs. Formula 400 is a step apart. A step ahead. Which is why we rightfully declare it to be tomorrow's breed of road car.

⬆ The Firebird Formula 400 was a way to circumvent the oppressive insurance premiums that came with the Trans Am package.

Plymouth and Dodge

Plymouth Road Runner Superbird

Plymouth 'Cuda 426

Dodge Challenger 426

Dodge Charger 440 Six Pack

Dodge Charger R/T 426 Street Hemi

Chrysler Corporation was on the upswing in the late 1960s, ending the decade far stronger than it had started it. Plymouth was the sales leader for Chrysler in total production, placing it just behind Chevrolet, Ford, and Pontiac throughout most of the decade. The year 1970 would prove to be a pinnacle year for Plymouth, with sales surpassing Pontiac for the first time in more than a decade. Plymouth production had remained steady while most of General Motors' product line was negatively impacted by a costly three-month-long strike.

Although beauty is in the eye of the beholder, Plymouth could be credited with creating both the most beautiful and the most homely muscle cars of 1970. The beauty was found in the new Barracuda design with its perfectly proportioned long nose/short deck styling. In contrast, the Plymouth Superbird was considered radical by many, but it was all in the name of aerodynamics for NASCAR superspeedways. Purpose-built, the Superbird was designed for two reasons: to lure Richard Petty back to Plymouth and to dominate NASCAR's superspeedways.

When most other cars had a distinctive grille area, the Superbird's air intake was hidden on the underside of its pointed nose cone. And as if that nose cone weren't distracting enough, the massive rear wing was visible to everyone except the driver, who couldn't see anything of it through the rearview mirror except the shadows it cast while driving. So radical were the Superbird, sold during the 1970 model year, and the Dodge Daytona, offered in 1969, that many remained unsold for years—into the mid-1970s in a few instances. That is, until potential buyers latched on to the future collectability of the winged cars. Both the Daytona and the Superbird's aerodynamic designs would blaze the trail for future car designs for decades to come, albeit not in such a radical way.

The Rapid Transit System was Plymouth's performance advertising campaign starting in 1970, two years following Dodge's Scat Pack marketing campaign initiated in 1968. The bold two-page magazine advertisements displayed the line product lineup in a desert environment. It included a Hemi 'Cuda, GTX, Fury GT, Road Runner, and 340 Duster with the slogan, "If you can't beat the system, join it."

The Dodge offerings during these years had their own following. Each Scat Pack Dodge would receive a decal on the rear side glass that showed a stylized bumble bee with spinning mag wheels and a V-8 motor on its back. The Scat Pack lineup for 1970 included the all-new Dodge Challenger, the Super Bee, the Charger R/T, the Coronet R/T, and the Dart Swinger 340.

Although both Plymouth and Dodge had their different models and marketing campaigns they shared the same powerplants. The performance buyer had a slew of engine options, spanning from 340 to 440 cubic inches and having one, two, or three carburetors. Both the Rapid Transit System and the Scat Pack offered the top-of-the-line 426 Hemi in each model in 1970 except for the small A-body Plymouth Duster and Dodge Dart Swinger, both of which were limited to the high-revving 340 small-block V-8.

The short period of 1969 to 1970 would provide the perfect marriage of industry-leading design and affordable high performance for the team from Highland Park, Michigan. And the 1970 model year, as it was for other manufacturers, would be considered the high-water mark of the first Golden Age of the Muscle Car.

But within just three years following the end of the 1970 model year, it would all come crashing down. First came Detroit's need to dedicate valuable corporate engineering resources to meet ever-increasing safety and emission standards, improving fleet fuel economy, changing consumer tastes, an insurance industry dedicated to making insurance unaffordable, especially for drivers under thirty, and finally in the fall of 1973, the first OPEC oil crisis.

But for one shining year, 1970, Mopar's high-performance Plymouth and Dodge lineup was without peer. It truly was the best of times to be an automotive enthusiast worshiping at the altar of high performance.

Plymouth Road Runner Superbird

AUTO WRITERS THROW AROUND the word "iconic" sometimes as if it were candy. And that is often the case with the 1970 Plymouth Road Runner Superbird, the second of Chrysler's winged warriors. It is the byproduct of that special era of NASCAR racing, when the participating manufacturers, Ford and Chrysler, left no stone unturned to gain an advantage on NASCAR's high-banked ovals. It started in 1969 when Ford (with the Ford Talladega and Mercury Cyclone Spoiler II) and Chrysler (with the Dodge Charger 500, Charger Daytona, and Plymouth Road Runner Superbird) built or outsourced the building of special limited-production, aerodynamically enhanced models to gain an advantage as the cars lapped at speeds approaching 200 miles per hour at both Daytona and NASCAR's newest superspeedway, Talladega.

Plymouth, after losing Richard Petty to Ford for the 1969 NASCAR season, had no immediate answer. It was left to Dodge with the Charger 500 and then the Daytona, to carry the corporate colors for the 1969 season, which resulted in a driver's championship for David Pearson and the manufacturers' championship for the Blue Oval.

For the 1970 season, Plymouth responded with its own winged warrior, the Plymouth Road Runner Superbird. But it was more than a rebadged version of the Dodge Charger Daytona. The car's trademark nose cone, which protruded 19 inches in front of the car's front fenders, was further refined from the one previously designed for the 1969 Dodge Charger for the Daytona. Around back is the car's distinctive wing. For many years the calculation of its height was said to be a closely guarded secret within Chrysler Corporation. Then in the 1990s a Chrysler engineer claimed that its height was to allow the trunk to open, a claim that was later debunked.

⬆ The rear-mounted adjustable wing on the 1970 Plymouth Road Runner Superbird towers 23 inches over the car's trunk lid.

↑ The 1970 Plymouth Road Runner Superbird was smaller and lighter than the 1969 Dodge Charger Daytona. The two scoops located on the top of each fender allowed more tire clearance when the car was lowered for NASCAR racing.

The real reason for its height? According to author Steve Lehto, who spoke with Chrysler engineer John Pointer, the truth was finally revealed. Pointer had an interesting backstory, having worked at Chrysler's missile division in Huntsville, Alabama, before moving over to the automotive group. Pointer was literally a rocket scientist and designed both cars' wings as well as their nose cones. There are subtle differences between the components on each car.

When parked side by side with a Daytona, the Superbird's "beak" is more pointed than the one installed on its corporate cousin. And around back, the supports for the Superbird's wing are shaped differently with a more pronounced rake.

But the height of the wing? The motivation was simple: to get the wing in clean air, above the turbulence generated by the air coming off the roof. That the trunk lid cleared the wing was simply a coincidence on both cars. NASCAR's only applicable rule in place at the time was that the trunk lid needed to be supported by OEM-style hinges. Before 1970, to homologate special production for the races sanctioned by its organization, NASCAR required that a specific number of units, five hundred for 1969, be built by all manufacturers. For the 1970 season NASCAR changed the rules to one for every two dealers in the United States. For Plymouth the minimum requirement was 1,920 Superbirds, which allowed Plymouth to entice Petty back to the flock. However, NASCAR rule changes limiting displacement for these aero cars to 305 cubic inches for the 1971 season would have rendered them uncompetitive. The 1970 NASCAR season was the aero cars' swan song.

The Superbird shown here is one of the reported 1,935 built for 1970. (Research shows claims by ex-Chrysler employees in interviews that as few as 1,300 or as many as

2,700 were built. But over the years Mopar experts have settled on 1,935 as the true production count. The numbers break down to 1,084 for the four-barrel 440, 716 for the six-barrel version of the 440, and just 135 for the 426 Hemi.)

With its Lemon Twist paint with the contrasting black vinyl top, this Road Runner Superbird is impossible to ignore, even when compared to the Dodge Charger Daytona. This is borne out when the cars are photographed together, nose to tail. Each has a distinctive profile.

The interior is what you would expect: a vinyl-trimmed front split-bench seat, black with silver accents from the Road Runner in this case, not the higher-spec materials from the GTX. The wood-trimmed pistol-grip Hurst shifter stands out in the sea of black. It's all very typical of what's found in countless 1968 to 1970 Dodge and Plymouth B-bodies.

In 2006 *Muscle Car Review* magazine created a controversial list of the fifty fastest muscle cars offered to the public based on quarter-mile times published in various magazines when the cars were new and still in full factory trim. A Hemi Superbird placed twelfth on the list with a quarter-mile time of 13.5 seconds and top speed of 105 miles per hour. A 1969 440 Six Pack Super Bee was seventeenth on the list with a time of 13.56 as per the August 1969 *Hot Rod* magazine test. The close proximity of these two quarter-mile times would lead one to believe the Superbird's aerodynamic differences were more effective for continuous high-speed racing than quick acceleration tests.

Although the Superbird was designed for NASCAR races, Ronnie Sox and Buddy Martin chose to drag race two versions in the early 1970s. One of those was equipped with the 426 Hemi and was called *The Boss*. Although it appeared to be a factory

The Plymouth Road Runner Superbird's huge rear spoiler hides the flush rear window treatment. All Road Runner Superbirds received a black vinyl top in order to hide the altered rear window plug.

Superbird, it did not have the traditional reverse-facing scoops on the top of each fender. The reason for the scoops was actually additional tire clearance when the car was lowered for NASCAR racing, so it is possible Sox and Martin choose to remove them for additional aero efficiency. The two Sox and Martin Superbirds were run in SS/E and SS/EA with an A-12 Six Pack–style hood scoop and was later run under the name *Super Chicken*.

Building the Superbird to satisfy the Plymouth dealers clamoring for their own version of the Daytona went far beyond installing the Charger's nose cone. The front fenders of the Road Runner were contoured differently than those found on the Daytona, so that wouldn't work. So a revised nose cone was developed.

The aerodynamic backlight (rear window), which was different from the one found on the Daytona, required that each Superbird have the optional vinyl roof installed to more easily conceal the modifications made for the installation of the unique glass to the sail panel (C-pillar flowing into the rear fenders). The design was approved under severe time constraints as the car needed to be ready for the Daytona 500 in February 1970. The concept was then sent off to subcontractor Creative Industries for production of the cars before January 1, 1970. Because it was introduced after the traditional fall new-model introductions, the Superbird does not appear in the 1970 Plymouth Belvedere (intermediates) dealership brochure, which covered the standard Road Runner, Belvedere, and GTX sedans, hardtops, station wagons, and convertibles. It wasn't even featured in the separate 1970 Rapid Transit System booklet. Like the Charger Daytona introduced the year previously, you had to be well connected with your local Chrysler-Plymouth dealer to know of its limited availability—only one was built for every other Chrysler-Plymouth dealership, which made them rare at the time.

➡ In the desert hills north of Palm Springs in the distance, the 1970 Plymouth Road Runner Superbird looks as if it's going 200 miles per hour.

What is hard to understand, five decades on with the six-figure price tags at auction over the last fifteen years for the most original or best-restored examples, is that the Superbird was originally a hard sell. The $4,298 base price was exorbitant for the time, and many had to be heavily discounted before they could be sold. There are many reports from the years following their 1970 introduction of Superbirds remaining unsold, languishing at the dealers where they were originally delivered. Some had their Superbird-specific parts and components removed and were sold as regular Road Runners.

Then came the 1973 OPEC oil embargo, which made a limited-production, 390-horsepower American supercar an almost impossible-to-sell used car. Can you imagine the sight of a High Impact–color Superbird waiting in a 1974 odd-even gas line?

Thankfully, of the almost two thousand Superbirds built in 1970 it's been reported that one thousand have survived. The high rate of survival is directly correlated to the reason they were hard to sell in the first place. The car's stand-out-in-the-crowd appearance saved many from the tragic fate of abandonment and neglect. The image of the car and often an owner's name were burned into the memories of young children who grew up seeing the winged warriors on the streets of their hometown. Many would later track down the cars they remembered and work to bring them out of their hiding places back into the public eyes. Don't be fooled by every Road Runner with a pointy nose and an oversized wing, though, as rising values have created countless clones built from more pedestrian Road Runners. The fact that Plymouth had the courage and foresight to create the Superbird in the first place is something to be thankful for.

The interior of the Superbird is pretty basic. Many were equipped with a bench seat rather than the optional bucket seats.

BFGoodrich radial T/A tires were not offered in-period but contribute to making this 1970 Plymouth Road Runner Superbird a much more comfortable drive than its original fiberglass-belted bias-ply tires.

The design for the wing on the 1970 Plymouth Road Runner Superbird is attributed to Gary Romberg, the ex-NASA engineer who contributed to the Saturn booster program that put Neil Armstrong on the Moon. In 1969 he moved to Chrysler where he had a long career. He passed away in early 2020.

SHAKER

⬆ The year 1970 was the first to officially include the massive Hemi engine in the E-body pony cars.

⬇ Hemi 'Cudas came with two different hood options: the standard dual-scoop 'Cuda hood and the shaker hood scoop sticking out of the flat hood. The hood scoop was either argent, as seen here, or finished in the body color.

OF ALL THE CARS IN THIS BOOK that can be called icons of the era, one must put the 1970 Plymouth Barracuda at the top of the list. Like the brand-new Challenger introduced that same year, it is blessed with what many say are perfect proportions—a high-water mark of the long-hood, short-deck genre pioneered by Ford's first Mustang in the spring of 1964.

Its exterior styling is credited to Plymouth studio chief John Herlitz, who—like his counterpart at Dodge, Carl Cameron, with the Challenger introduced that year—crafted a tailored suit for Chrysler's all-new E-body platform that has stood the test of time. In fact, fifty years after its introduction, it can be considered timeless.

Like its Dodge counterpart, Plymouth's variation of the E-body platform was proportionally wider than competitors in the pony-car class. In fact you can consider the Barracuda as something of a preview of the volume-selling Dodge and Plymouth B-body intermediates already in their final development pipeline to debut the following fall for the 1971 model year.

The Barracuda was not always a design benchmark. Introduced two weeks before Ford's Mustang in April 1964, the first Barracuda was nothing more than a Valiant with what could be called a fishbowl rear backlight, which gave the car somewhat awkward fastback proportions that couldn't hide its origins. The original Mustang, itself based on Ford's compact Falcon platform, got an all-new body design that disguised its economy-car origins with a 2+2 design featuring its signature styling element, its long hood combined with a short rear overhang that gave the car a sporty look. The Valiant-based Barracuda looked exactly like what it was, a Valiant with a big rear window.

The second-generation Barracuda, introduced in the fall of 1966 as a 1967 model, came off much better. Some called its styling European-inspired, and that was certainly true for the fastback version. The 1967–1968 Barracuda was offered in three body styles: the fastback, a pretty coupe version, and the obligatory convertible, going head-to-head with Mustang's lineup. While it sold better than its predecessor, it was no match for the Mustang and faced competition from GM's Chevrolet Camaro and Pontiac Firebird (a midyear launch) and in 1968, AMC's sporty Javelin.

Hot 'Cudas came in three distinct flavors for 1970: the small-block 340-powered cars, which included the 'Cuda 340 with a single four-barrel carb along with the AAR 'Cuda (for Dan Gurney's All American Racers) with the three-carb setup; the 440 six-barrel; and, of course, Plymouth's own version of the legendary Street Hemi, now offered for a fifth year. All were part of the Rapid Transit System, a group of American-built supercars that, five decades on, has now passed into legend.

◤ The new-for-1970 'Cuda model had an aggressive appearance with a single headlight on each side of the grille. The optional road lamps came standard with clear lenses for the North American market.

◢ Although the 'Cuda package is called out on the back of the car, there is no engine designation located anywhere other than on the hood or hood scoop.

All-American: The AAR 'Cuda

WHEN IT COMES TO SELECTING the best-balanced Plymouth 1970 E-body, many point to the small-block AAR 'Cuda. Designed to accommodate the 426 and 440 big-blocks. The approach came with a cost—weight.

The entry-level performance model in Plymouth's E-body lineup was the 'Cuda 340. The 340 block was some 150 pounds lighter than the 426 Hemi. At $3,164 for the two-door hardtop model (the convertible carried a base price of $3,433), the 'Cuda 340 was the performance bargain in Plymouth's 1970 lineup.

For 1970, Dan Gurney took an offer from Plymouth to campaign the all-new Barracuda in the SCCA's Trans-Am series. The AAR team ran destroked 305-cubic-inch versions of the 340 V-8 like the corresponding Dodge Challenger T/A, producing a reported 450 horsepower.

The AAR 'Cuda fell under expanded homologation rules. Plymouth needed to produce 2,500 units by the first race of the season on April 17, 1970. All 2,724 units were produced in just five weeks and configured with factory options as well as a unique appearance package.

⬆ The AAR 'Cuda had several unique features differentiating it from the standard 340 Cudas, including the fiberglass hood with integrated scoop, flat black hood treatment, laser side stripes, side exhaust, rear spoiler, and rear-mounted antenna.

The 340 V-8 was an available regular production option for the 1970 'Cuda but did not include the 290-horsepower Six-Pack carburetor setup unless ordered in the AAR package. The AAR also included a lightweight fiberglass hood with center scoop and hood pins. The massive hood and fender tops were painted flat black to reduce reflection. Strobe-style stripes in 3M reflective black decals flanked each side and finished in a red, white, and blue AAR decal on each rear quarter.

The rear end received a low-profile trunk-lip spoiler in place of the 'Cuda Go-Wing pedestal spoiler. Optional road lamps were located under the chrome front bumper, and the package was finished off with side-exiting exhaust with trumpet-style tips exposed in front of each rear wheel. The heavy-duty suspension included front and rear sway bars along with higher-rated rear shocks that raised the rear end, giving a menacing rake. Each AAR 'Cuda was equipped with standard power front disc brakes with 15×7 road wheels and E60×15 Goodyear white letter tires up front with G60×15 tires on the rear.

The street version's 340 advertised 275 horsepower, an unsuccessful attempt to fool insurance adjusters. The AAR 'Cuda sported three two-barrel Holley carbs atop an Edelbrock aluminum manifold. Buyers could choose either the robust TorqueFlite 727 three-speed automatic or a four-speed manual. Either could be combined with a Sure-Grip limited-slip differential with the standard 3.23:1 rear axle ratio or optional 3.55:1 or 3.91:1 gears in the Performance Axle package.

Like all the 1970 Barracudas, the interior was all new, owing nothing to the 1967–1969 cars that preceded it. Most 'Cudas came equipped with bucket seats with vinyl trim. Who doesn't have a memory of jumping behind the wheel wearing shorts on a hot summer's day and burning one's thighs?

The AAR package was not shown in 1970 Barracuda dealership brochures or widely distributed marketing materials. Retail price for a base AAR 'Cuda was a muscle-car bargain at only $3,966.

1970 'Cuda Big-Blocks

ONE OF THE RAREST OF ALL the E-body cars by virtue of its pilot-build status is the V-code 440 Six-Pack owned (at the time of the book's writing) by Patti and Dana Mecum. As VIN 100004, there is no doubt as to its pedigree. This car sports the now iconic shaker scoop.

V-code signifies that this Alpine White convertible is equipped with the Super Commando 440 V-8 with the Holley three-carb setup, producing an advertised 390 horsepower, able to propel the car from 0 to 60 in under 6 seconds with the quarter mile coming up in 14.04 seconds at a trap speed of 100 miles per hour. Inside, by 'Cuda standards, this car is equipped for luxury as well as performance. Its options include leather bucket seats, power windows, and the top audio offering: an AM/eight-track stereo system. Three significant performance options include the robust Dana 60 differential, the Track Pak, and a 26-inch radiator.

A fully optioned car with this specification, if all the boxes ticked, would have sold for nearly $5,000 in 1970, the price of a Chevrolet Corvette in that era. In 1970 just thirteen more V-code four-speed 'Cuda Six Pack convertibles like this one rolled off the Hamtramck assembly.

Another take on Chrysler's versatile E-body platform is the second 'Cuda featured here, a 1970 hardtop in Plum Crazy, again powered by a V-code 440 Six-Pack. Lacking a vinyl top, it best illustrates the purity of what emerged from John Herlitz's Plymouth studio. Herlitz's son Todd, born a few years after the car was built, offered up these retrospective comments: "If you were to ask my dad . . . he would tell you that although he is generally credited with the design of that car, every car design is a real team effort, and no one person gets the credit. I think he was always a little uncomfortable that he was known as 'the designer' of the 1970 Barracuda."

Of course when it comes to the pinnacle of the evolution of the 1970–1974 E-body cars, one stands at the top: the Street Hemi–powered cars. While it's hard to believe, knowing what we know now, the Hemi-powered cars were not an easy sell, with just 652 hardtops and 14 convertibles finding buyers in 1970. These were split between 377 TorqueFlite three-speed automatics and 289 New Process A-833 heavy-duty four-speed cars. The rarest reported combination? Of the 14 Hemi convertibles, just 5 came equipped with the A-833 manual.

In the fall of 1969 when the 'Cuda was introduced, a 0-to-60 sprint of 5.8 seconds was top tier—especially considering the tire technology of the day. You could drive all this off the floor of your local dealership for less than $4,500 ($30,000 in 2020 dollars).

⬆ When equipped with the 440 six barrel, 390-horspower V-8, the 1970 'Cuda could sprint from 0 to 60 in just 5.9 seconds according to *Motor Trend* when they tested the car for the May 1970 issue.

Dodge Challenger 426

⬆ Blasting through the Rocky Mountains west of Denver on a 2008 trip that celebrated the return of the Dodge Challenger to the Dodge lineup—what a perfect excuse to travel with a friend with a 1970 Go Mango Dodge Challenger R/T 426 Hemi.

IN THE LATE 1960S Dodge was at something of a crossroads. While it was Chrysler's full-line division, it had totally missed the exploding pony-car market, twice. In 1964, when the Plymouth Barracuda beat the Ford Mustang to the marketplace by two weeks, Dodge did not offer a corresponding model. All it had to offer was a spec'd-up version of the two-door Dart compact, the GT, in a sporty two-door hardtop and convertible, each with bucket seats and available console, much like the Mustang but with less style.

Its first answer was the midsized Charger, introduced in 1966. Based on the intermediate-sized Coronet, it missed the mark set by the Mustang by a wide margin. It didn't even help that the first-generation Charger was equipped with what is quite possibly the most outstanding interior of its time—four individual bucket seats with an available full-length center console along with unique (and costly) electroluminescent gauges—and a wide engine bay that could accommodate any engine Chrysler offered, including the street version of the legendary 426 Hemi. The public hardly noticed.

And a year later, when Plymouth introduced the second-generation A-body Barracuda in hardtop, Italian-inspired fastback, and convertible models (all which shared underpinnings with the compact Valiant and Dart) no comparably appealing Dodge showed up for the contest.

With the three-year development cycles common at the time, Dodge missed two generations of pony cars. The second, shaped by Mustang, Cougar, Camaro, midyear Pontiac Firebird, and Barracuda, had transformed the car market since 1967. As the new kid on the playground in 1970, Dodge had a lot to prove.

The Challenger's original benchmark was the 1967 Mercury Cougar, Ford's upscale version of the class-leading Mustang. William Brownlie was the vice president for styling and product planning for Dodge at the time. Brownlie did then what Dodge might have done a car generation before—he coordinated with the Plymouth group, then planning its third-generation Barracuda.

Dodge's original goal of pursuing a more luxurious pony car shifted to a more aggressive approach when the restyled 1968 Dodge Charger sold three times as well as the division had expected. It was reportedly one of Brownlie's sketches that would form the foundation of what, fifty years later, would become recognized as one of the most iconic pony-car designs of its era. Another piece of the development puzzle that influenced the design was the fact that the Challenger, along with the Barracuda, would share much of its underlying platform—especially the all-important cowl area and its front subframe—with the upcoming 1971 B-body replacements for the Dodge Charger and Coronet and the Plymouth Satellite. That broader platform would make for an engine bay capable of accepting any engine in the Chrysler family, including the 426 Hemi and 440.

When it was introduced in the fall of 1969 as a 1970 model, the E-body Challenger hit all the marks, owing to Dodge's "Have it your way" marketing strategy. The Challenger offered a hardtop and convertible, two trim levels, and several powertrains, everything from a commuter slant six to the Hemi and Six Pack big-blocks focused on short, fast trips of a quarter mile each.

A bit of the original Mercury inspiration did show through in the Challenger's wheelbase. Just as the Cougar's was longer than the Mustang's, the Challenger's 110-inch wheelbase was 2 inches longer than that of its corporate cousin, the

⬇ This was the view that most drivers had of a 1970 Hemi Challenger—its distinctive full-width taillights.

Plymouth's Barracuda. Two models were offered initially, the standard model and the better-equipped R/T. At just $300 more than the base model priced at $2,851, the R/T added the 383-cubic-inch, 335-horsepower V-8, heavy-duty Rallye suspension, F70×14 tires, and Rallye instrument cluster with a 150-mile-per-hour speedometer and an 8,000-rpm tachometer. (To give one an idea of the bargain pricing of the 1970 Challenger, when adjusted for five decades of inflation the base Challenger today would cost $20,000 today with just $22,000 for the upmarket R/T model.)

Among the Challenger's many guises was the oft-overlooked Challenger T/A, Dodge's spring 1970 homologation entry into the Trans-Am sales sweepstakes. The T/A's development had been spurred on by Dan Gurney's All American Racers team, which for 1970 was running a Challenger for Sam Posey since Mercury had abandoned its support for factory-backed entries.

Dodge's T/A was something of a hybrid. Because the division had no ready V-8 that would meet the Trans-Am series' 5-liter, 305-cubic-inch limit, the racing T/As ran the same destroked 340s homologated for the Barracudas in previous years. For its street version, Dodge went with its available 340-cubic-inch V-8. This engine was equipped with three two-barrel carburetors, producing a grossly underrated 290 horsepower (like the Mustang Boss 302 and the Camaro Z/28).

The production Challenger T/As, of which 2,142 were built—many in the High Impact colors that were the rage in 1970—have become among the most coveted Mopars of the era. As the price of its big-block stablemates has skyrocketed over the years, especially at high-profile auctions, the previously overlooked T/A models have caught the attention of Mopar enthusiasts. And like other Trans-Am–inspired competitors, the T/A provides one of the best driving experiences of any pony car from that era. While its engine bay can accommodate any Mopar big-block, the lighter 340 V-8 offers significantly better handling characteristics with little penalty in straightline speed. The numbers from contemporary road tests speak for themselves: 0 to 60 in 5.9 seconds and quarter-mile times falling into the mid-14-second range.

But if power is to define the pinnacle of the first muscle-car era, the discussion must move to the two bulls in the room, the Challengers powered by the 426 Hemi or the 440 Six Pack. Despite more displacement, the 440 Six Pack often stands in the shadow of the 426 Elephant Hemi, and in a way that's unfortunate. It has a character all its own, courtesy of the three-carb induction setup first introduced on the 1969 Dodge Super Bee.

The 440 Six Pack arose in large part from Chrysler's desire to have a less temperamental engine for its high-performance street cars than the all-conquering but very expensive Street Hemi. For this, it turned to two well-respected suppliers, Edelbrock and Holley. Edelbrock supplied Chrysler with a high-rise aluminum intake manifold, while Holley provided three center-hung float 2300 two-barrel carbs. There could have been a lot of air—1,000 cfm to be exact. Chrysler's engineers redesigned the setup so that each carb was an equal distance from its respective port, eliminating the possibility of any one cylinder going lean.

Introduced first in the 1969 Super Bee, the triple-carb 440 spread across the 1969 B-body offerings for 1970, including the newly introduced 1970 Challenger. And 2,035 of the six-carb monsters found their way under the hoods of 1970 Challenger R/Ts.

↑↑ Dodge's stylists used every opportunity to add timeless details to the Challenger, in this case its fuel filler door.

↑ Although the BFGoodrich radial T/A tires weren't available for 1970, the classic Mopar five-lug Rallye wheels were part of the T/A package.

←← Just south of the Bonneville Salt Flats in Utah, a reflective pool along I-40 gives this Mopar E-Body another opportunity to show off its classic lines, which have stood the test of time.

⬆ Dodge offered the 1970 Challenger in many different flavors. It could be ordered with a mild 225-cubic-inch slant-six cylinder engine to a wild 426-cubic-inch Hemi mill.

The rarest combination seems to be the thirty-eight automatic convertibles that rolled off the Hamtramck, Michigan, assembly line.

The 440 Six Pack–equipped Challengers could rip off the 0-to-60 benchmark in under 6 seconds while covering the quarter mile in just 13.62 seconds at 104 miles per hour, according to a road test published in the November 1969 issue of *Car Craft* magazine. In R/T trim, the Challenger ran $3,516 for the hardtop, $3,785 for the convertible.

When the pinnacle muscle cars for 1970 is considered, the Hemi-powered Challengers stand atop the pyramid with the LS6-powered SS454 Chevrolet Chevelles and the Mustang Boss 429s. The 426 Hemi engines are mentioned in other sections of this book, as it was found in other B- and E-body Mopars. From its introduction in 1964, powering Richard Petty's first win at Daytona, and its introduction in street trim in 1966 in the B-body intermediates, the second-generation Hemi stood atop Mopar's engine hierarchy.

For 1970 its availability spread to Chrysler's new E-body pony cars, the Challenger and Barracuda. The cost of the Hemi plus its mandatory options was staggering for the time—$1,228, bringing the base-price Challenger R/T to $4,056. The Hemi came equipped with the robust three-speed TorqueFlite three-speed automatic or a four-speed manual with a Hurst pistol-grip shifter. Noteworthy was that when the Hemi or the 440 Six Pack was paired with the four-speed, a 9.75-inch Dana 60 rear axle was included. Clearly Chrysler's engineers and marketing people knew what to expect: excessive warranty claims if the Dana 60 wasn't part of the manual transmission package.

In the Challenger, the Hemi provided the performance numbers that one would expect—0 to 60 in under 6 seconds, with the quarter mile a 14-second dash reaching 104 miles per hour.

In the years that followed, as cars were lost to mishaps and the ravages of time, few fans could foresee the grail of the muscle-car era the Challenger would become. In the early 2000s, as those who had raced or dreamed about Dodge's hard-punching pony car in their youth found themselves successful businessmen and entrepreneurs, they reached into their pasts and their stock portfolios and threw dollars at Challenger (and its peers) in heaps no Chrysler executive ever dared to dream possible. Suddenly the most desirable Challengers were worth more than the houses whose garages they slumbered in, and none more so than Hemi-powered beasts from 1970. The new kid on the playground ultimately made good—very good.

From new, Dodge's pony car met a strong reception with first-year sales of 83,032 units. While this trailed the class-leading Mustang, it did best the 72,000 sales tallied by Mercury's Cougar, Dodge's initial development target. But that was to be as good as sales would get for the Challenger. As with most other pony cars, production went south quickly as the pressures of emission and safety standards, as well as rising insurance rates, weighed down the segment and crushed performance capabilities. The drops were stark. Sales fell 60 percent for 1971, the final year of the convertible, to just 29,883 cars. For 1972, they slipped to 26,663. There was a slight rebound to 32,596 in 1973 before the plummet to 16,437 for the final short-run 1974 model. In the end, the car's short stint on the scene seems to have helped its desirability and boosted Chrysler's sales of muscular vehicles in the twenty-first century.

Dodge Charger 440 Six Pack

IN THE THIRD YEAR of its then current cycle, the Dodge Charger's styling had aged well. Sales, however, which started at 96,100 in 1968 and dropped slightly to 89,199 in 1969, had fallen by almost half to 49,768 in 1970, likely impacted by the introduction of the Challenger. The hotter two-door versions of the midsized 1970 Coronet also impacted sales.

What the Charger may have lacked in terms of fresh sheet metal for 1970, however, it more than made up for under the hood. Like its B-body counterparts—the Plymouth Road Runner and Satellite and the Dodge Super Bee and Coronet—the Charger's big-block options included the 383, 426, and 440, offering an advertised 375 horsepower for the 383 to 425 horsepower for the top-dog Hemi.

The car that garnered the attention of the enthusiasts was the new-for-1970 390-horsepower Six Pack 440, featuring a trio of Holley two-barrel carbs. According to reports at the time, the three-by-two setup was less temperamental that the dual quads on the Hemi. But anyone who has tried to keep three deuces in tune might question that claim. One area where the 440 had an advantage over the Hemi is that its torque came on 800 rpm lower, contributing to its ability to get off the mark smartly.

While its Plymouth counterparts were attractive, especially the top-of-the-line GTX (the Charger's most direct corporate competitor), in the eye of many design critics the purity of the 1968–1970 Chargers has never been surpassed. What one must recognize is how difficult it is for stylists to get proportion laid out over such a large car. It's one thing to get sporty long hood, short deck proportions to work on a smaller pony car, but it's something else altogether to get it to work on an intermediate-sized two-door hardtop. On a design with so many interesting angles—such as the reverse scoops covering the fender scallops on the R/T models and the flying-buttress C-pillars—the 1968–1970 Charger was a standout. Of course, these C-pillars wreaked havoc on NASCAR aerodynamics, as noted earlier, but for a car destined for the

↑ Blair's Speed Shop in Pasadena is a Southern California hot rod institution. Founded by Don Blair in 1946, it survives to this day.

1970 Dodge Charger.
Stands out with the "in" crowd.

This one will turn heads wherever it goes. It's that kind of car. The kind of car you buy when you're ready for a sharp-looking sports type with a little more room. A car with a continental-type front bumper that encompasses the grille. Hidden headlights. Rallye instrument panel. Rallye Suspension. Racing gas cap. Bucket seats, or bench. Charger offers both. Either way, Charger gives you an awful lot of car for a surprisingly low price. And for a few bucks more, you can have the Charger SE (Special Edition) or the Charger R/T. Take your pick. If you're waiting for an invitation . . . this is it. Drop in. Shape out. Stand out. With the "in" crowd. 1970 Dodge Charger.

If you don't want another same old brand-new car . . . you could be DODGE MATERIAL.

⬆ In the final year of its three-year model run, Dodge tried presenting its midsized muscle car to a more sophisticated buyer, as seen in this 1970 ad. Could you be Dodge Material?

⬇ One of the signature design elements of the 1968–1970 Dodge Chargers is shown here from the rear view: the flying buttress C-pillar design with the recessed backlight (rear window).

street, they were perfection, especially when mated with the locking chrome fuel filler cap mounted on the top of the driver's-side rear fender.

If the design of the 1968–1970 Charger fell short in any respect, it was on the inside. There was nothing wrong; it's just that the interior lacked the drop-dead gorgeous design elements of the 1966–1967 Chargers. In place of the previous generation's aircraft-inspired design, the new interiors were utterly conventional with an attractive, well-styled dash and the company's full complement of gauges. (The gauges set apart Chrysler's interiors of this era, especially when compared with Ford and GM.) It's not hard to speculate on why the first generation's costly four bucket seats with a full-length center console were eliminated, just like the ultracool electroluminescent gauge cluster found on the 1966–1967 Chargers, but we'll never know for certain, as the designers responsible have long since retired.

When the 1970 models were introduced in the fall of 1969, the bold new color palette was the big news visually: Plum Crazy, Sublime, Go Mango, Hemi Orange, and Top Banana Yellow. The example pictured on these pages, a Charger R/T 440 Six Pack in Go Mango, ticks every box. The Six Pack 440 propels the car from 0 to 60 in just 5.6 seconds and covers the quarter mile in 14.2 seconds, going through the trap at 98.6 miles per hour according to contemporary road tests.

On the inside this 1970 Charger R/T is equipped with front bucket seats with perforated leather seating surfaces and a center console. The four-speed manual transmission is stirred with a Hurst pistol-grip shifter. Being that this is an intermediate-sized car, the interior is spacious, and the rear seat can easily handle a pair of adults, or three in a pinch. Like many Charger R/T models, this one is comprehensively equipped with power front disc brakes, power steering, and an AM radio (AM/FM was available).

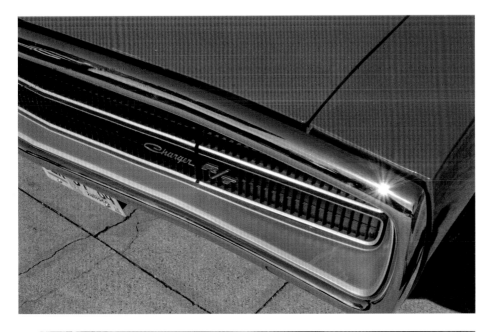

⬆⬆ The concealed headlights of the 1968–1970 Dodge Chargers gave all versions (except for the special Dodge Charger 500 models with fixed, exposed headlights) a very clean look up front.

⬆ The new-for-1970 440 Six Pack option, featuring three two-barrel carburetors and producing 390-horsepower, was a popular option, costing far less than the 426 Hemi.

⬈ The R/T designated Road and Track package included the 15x7 rally wheels that were shared with many other Dodge and Plymouth performance models.

➡ The 1970 Charger offered many comfort and appearance options that included bucket seats, a six-way option, power windows, and a console.

⬆ This Charger has both the R/T and the SE options. Car enthusiasts had to look close to quickly size up a potential street competitor. The R/T equals a performance package, the SE package was luxury-based, but the little silver rectangle on the front edge of the fender told the real story. This car is equipped with a Hemi.

IF THE 390-HORSEPOWER 440 wasn't enough, like with other Mopar B-bodies you could specify the optional 426-cubic-inch Street Hemi for the Charger. With its dual-quad setup, it produced an advertised 425 horsepower. It was a very rare option, finding itself factory-installed under the hood of just 112 1970 Chargers, 56 with the three-speed TorqueFlite automatic transmission and another 56 equipped with the four-speed manual gearbox. It could accelerate from 0 to 60 in 6 seconds flat (some magazines in 1970 turned in sub-6-second times) and cover the quarter mile in 13.5 seconds with a trap speed of 105 miles per hour. It was rare to see top speeds stated in road tests at the time, but quick use of a slide rule (remember those?) will tell you that a Hemi-powered 1970 Dodge Charger in factory tune should be able to break through 130 miles per hour on Goodyear Polyglas GT F60×15 tires.

The Hemi-powered four-speed cars got one special upgrade, the super-robust Dana 60 Sure-Grip 8.75-inch rear end. With an available final drive ratio of 4.10:1, this was the setup to be specified for maximum acceleration from a standing start, especially for the quickest quarter-mile times. Of course, it was capable of showing its taillights to almost any stoplight grand prix opponent.

There were also two unusual (for the time) options offered for the 1970 Chargers: a sliding steel sunroof requiring the optional vinyl roof and leather-trimmed seating surfaces standard on the SE model. What's not known is just how many 440 Six Pack and 426 Hemi cars were equipped with the SE option. One option not available on 426 Hemi-equipped cars was factory-installed air-conditioning, due to the air compressor's limited RPM capacity.

When the last 1970 Chargers rolled down the assembly line in the summer of 1970, an era was coming to a close. Increasingly stringent emission regulations, the coming of low-lead gasoline, and ever-increasing insurance rates would soon bring down the curtain of the first muscle-car era. But the 1968–1970 Chargers, the 1970 models especially, ensured that the Golden Age of the Muscle Car went out on a high note.

⬇ The large Dodge Charger engine bay provides ample space for the elephant Hemi motor. Even with sufficient room, air-conditioning was not available with the Hemi motor.

▲ The SE option provided for a luxurious interior. Hurst designed a special shifter that had several bends to reach through the console and keep the driver from having to lean forward while shifting.

▼▼ This Charger is a heavily optioned model and had a factory sticker price north of $5,000. If you wanted a top-end muscle car in 1970, they were available if you could afford the payments and insurance. The rarity of these cars shows that few could afford them.

▲ A 1970 Charger R/T SE with Hemi motor is one of the most sought after collector cars today. Few were manufactured and many did not survive a life of abuse. Finding a restored example can prove difficult, with only a handful offered for sale at any time.

AMC

AMC was looking to create another high-profile car for 1970. Vice president of design Richard Teague recognized the value that image cars such as the 1969 SC/Rambler had created in the enthusiast press.

The Rambler name was retired in 1969, replaced by the new Hornet. The Hornet was selected to become the 1970 performance model to be named the Machine, with either the 360 or the 401 V-8. To date no historic photos have been discovered, but we unearthed a Ditzler paint-chart dated September 1969 identifying 1970 Electric Blue poly as an accent color on the lower rocker and hood of a new high-performance Hornet—identical to the color and design aspects on the 1970 Rebel Machine (color code 25A).

In 1970, the 390-cubic-inch engine was still AMC's largest. It is often incorrectly referred to as a big-block. However, weighing in at about 500 pounds, even the largest AMC V-8s clearly fit into a small-block category. The biggest difference from other engines of that dimension was that an AMC 390 produced 425 foot-pounds of torque, which was competitive with most big-blocks. The 1970 engines differed from the 1967–1969 design due to an additional deck height of 0.016 inch, allowing for larger displacement. The 290 version grew to 304 cubic inches; the 343 grew to 360 cubic inches; and the 390 stayed the same for 1970. AMC's new blocks also have bolts in place at the bottom design of previous years to help resolve head-gasket issues. Head design was also improved with expanded dog-leg exhaust ports.

↑↗→ AMC carried over the patriotic theme from the seven different factory-sponsored racing programs. There were five different factory red, white, and blue painted cars from AMC.

THE YEAR 1970 WAS PIVOTAL for AMC. A UAW strike would have a serious negative impact on both sales and profitability for the struggling manufacturer. It would also be the last year for both the two-seat version of the AMX and the intermediate-sized Rebel model line. On October 16, 1969, AMC Marketing VP Bill McNeeley encouraged by the previous year's expanded sales of the SC/Rambler, sent out a press release announcing the new Rebel Machine.

The same 390 was used in both the AMX and the Rebel Machine, with only two factory upgrades. The Rebel Machine had different intake and exhaust manifolds from the standard AMC 390 engine used for the other models. Oddly the improved intake remained a heavy cast dual-plane unit, as AMC chose not to use the lighter aftermarket aluminum Edelbrock RB4 intake that was listed in the AMC Group 19 catalog. The exhaust manifolds were also a special free-flow design that would resemble the later cast models used on AMC V-8s. This added 15 horsepower to the standard 390 engine, bringing the rating to 340 horsepower—the most powerful, as measured by gross horsepower, of any AMC V-8 in the company's history.

The Rebel Machine package was based on the company's intermediate platform (which was stretched to underpin the full-size Ambassador) and was lighter and slightly smaller than the Plymouth Road Runner. The Rebel two-door hardtop had been given a revised roofline for 1970 that provided more of a fastback profile than previous years. This redesign also eliminated the two-door post version. Building on this change, the Rebel Machine package included special larger 15×7 styled-steel wheels with permanently installed stainless-steel trim rings. AMC added stiffer rear coil springs, which produced a slightly raked profile that was a common look for the time. The side of the

car was devoid of external trim and three-dimensional emblems, with the only cast emblem being the *REBEL* lettering on the leading driver's-side edge of the hood and centered across the massive rear bumper.

The lack of side trim was obscured by paint details running along the bright white body. A bright blue line ran around the lower edge of the car. High on the sides ran a parallel red line that widened slightly from front to back before cutting across the trunk, where it sandwiched a white line against a blue one for a patriotic trio of red, white, and blue striping. Up front, the hood was primarily the same bright blue with white side edges. In the center of the hood was an overwidth box hood scoop with two wide intake ports. The back of the scoop had an integrated tachometer facing the driver that was impossible to read at night or during inclement weather. *The Machine* decals were applied to the upper trailing edge of each front fender, the right edge of the trunk lid, and the interior glove-box door.

The Rebel Machine debuted before the automotive press during the NHRA World Finals at Dallas International Motor Speedway on October 25, 1969. AMC provided ten identical white, blue, and red cars that were specially prepared for the event, used by NHRA officials during the race and to escort Hurst's Linda Vaughn, Miss Hurst Golden Shifter. Although Hurst was not directly involved with the construction of "the Machine" for AMC, it did have a part in the design aspects of the car. Vaughn and her Hurstettes were photographed in hippie-style clothing carrying around signs stating "Up with the Rebel Machine." The slogan was a play on the words used in a common antiwar protest slogan, "Down with the war in Vietnam."

AMC continued the tongue-in-cheek introduction theme by apologetically claiming 14.49 at 93.00 miles per hour in the official press release of the event, stating, "The Rebel Machine is not as fast on the getaway as a 427 Corvette or even a Hemi, but it is faster on the getaway than a Volkswagen, a slow freight train, and your old man's Cadillac!" After the introduction festivities, some of the Rebel Machine models were prominently displayed in local AMC dealership showrooms in the Dallas–Fort Worth area.

☙ Rebel Machine's rear appearance does not include the spoilers, window slats, or flat black paint treatment common on many other muscle cars in 1970.

⬇ Rebel Machine carried the red, white, and blue theme from American Motors racing teams into dealer showrooms and onto the streets of America.

The first few hundred cars made were identical, with the 25A paint code Frost White, Electric Blue, and Matador Red paint treatment. After the initial production, the Machine package could be ordered in any production color, without the bold side stripes, and with most factory options. The standard package was the 390-cubic-inch, 340-horsepower motor with either a four-speed manual transmission with the Hurst shifter or a floor-console-mounted automatic. Bucket seats were mandatory, as were power front disc brakes, factory handling package, and power steering. AMC included its limited-slip rear option, labeled as Twin Grip with the Machine's stock rear gear ratio of 3.54:1, the only factory option being 3.91:1. Ratios from 2.87 to 5.00 were available over the counter for those who wanted to dial in a particular sweet spot. Unlike the previous year's SC/Rambler package, factory-installed air-conditioning and a tilt steering wheel were available options.

The result of having more color choices and options available for the Machine created an increase in sales for the Rebel over the previous year's SC/Rambler. A total of 1,936 units were built, with an estimated half of them in the white, blue, and red paint scheme designated by 25A on the driver's door tag. Some of the other most sought-after colors included the Big Bad Green, Blue, and Orange hues available for 1970.

Equipped with the factory four-speed with a Hurst shifter, the Rebel Machine was powerful in a straight line but felt bigger than it was when cornering. The biggest deficiency was the coil-spring rear suspension, which made the car handle more like a station wagon than a performance car.

The white, blue, and red color scheme has remained more popular than the single-color versions, consistently commanding a 25 percent premium. The most desirable examples are equipped with factory four-speed, tilt steering wheel, and air-conditioning.

⬆⬆ The Rebel Machine's factory hood scoop incorporated a tachometer for the driver. Similar to the Pontiac hood-mounted tach, it was hard to read during inclement weather.

⬆ The Rebel Machine package included heavy-duty 15×7 steel wheels to improve handling. The wheels had a pressed-on trim ring that trapped road salt and dirt. Finding a set of these wheels in good condition today can be a challenge at a restorer.

🔻 Only the red, white, and blue Rebel Machines received the matching front seat folding armrest.

➡ The Rebel name first appeared on an AMC sedan in 1956, and it was last used by AMC in 1970.

🖤 The Rebel Machine engine was identical to the 390 used in the AMX. It received a 15-horsepower upgrade through the use of improved free-flow intake and exhaust manifolds.

⬇ Although AMC did not offer an eight-track option built into the factory Rebel radio, they did have a dealer-installed Motorola underdash unit as seen here.

⬆ This steering wheel was used for the Rebel, Javelin, and AMX, with each one having its own unique center medallion.

Interestingly, the Machine package continued into 1971 on the two-door body that was now called the Matador. For 1971 it required either the Z-code 401 or the P-code 360 four-barrel motor. As in 1970, it required both power front disc brakes and power steering and included the handling package. It was available with the floor-mounted four-speed, floor-mounted automatic, or column-mounted three-speed automatic.

The Matador had no outside designation showing the Machine package—no hood-scoop emblems or striping to help identify it. There have only been a handful of 1971 models discovered, all of which came with the factory 15×7 Machine wheel option. It would require a build sheet or window sticker to prove any additional 1971 Machine package cars as factory-built.

THE 1969 TRANS-AM SERIES continued into the fall of 1969 after the 1970 cars had been introduced. The Kaplan Javelin team finished second in the series for 1969, ahead of Ford but trailing Chevrolet. To celebrate this solid showing, AMC chose to release a special-edition Javelin to represent the race cars but in street trim. One hundred red-white-and-blue Javelins were built in September of 1969 and sold directly to the public. It was difficult to paint the special tricolor scheme, which required the Matador Red bodies to be pulled off the line and masked for two additional colors. The clean racing look of the car meant that the standard SST 4-inch-tall lower rocker moldings were eliminated from the build process.

The standard Javelin SST was equipped with a 390-cubic-inch, 325-horsepower engine—up 10 horsepower from the previous year due to the addition of ram air. This was achieved even with a slight reduction in compression from 10.2:1 to a flat 10.0:1. All were specially painted red, white, and blue with the black vinyl interior just like the successful Kaplan Javelin Trans-Am racing team car driven by George Follmer. All included the Borg Warner T-10 factory four-speed and Hurst shifter, power steering, power front disc brakes, and handling package, with factory 140-mile-per-hour speedometer and tachometer. Wheels were the standard 14×6 Magnum 500s painted in the gray speckle paint matched to Goodyear Polyglass white-letter F70×14 tires. Included was a special Group 19 rear adjustable spoiler, as used in the 1969 Trans-Am series by Kollmer, and a replica fiberglass front spoiler.

↑ An estimated one hundred Trans-Am AMC Javelins were built. All the cars included the 390-cubic-inch V-8. The manufacturer suggested retail price (MSRP) of the Trans-Am Javelin was $3,995.

AMC sent a memo to the dealers that due to the limited number of Trans-Am Javelins built, they could order a similar car in white and duplicate the Trans-Am paint scheme and options. For this reason, identifying an actual factory-built car requires knowing a car's details and history. The serial number of all 1967 and newer American Motors cars contain codes for the engine, transmission, and body style. Additionally on each 1970 American Motors car, the driver's door received a serial-number decal with the month of manufacture as well as a separate metal door tag that included the factory paint color and the sequence number for when that the car was assembled. This can be verified with production numbers to identify the week it was manufactured to correspond with the early release of this option package.

The factory-assembled Trans-Am package cars all received a "00" paint code designation on the driver's door data tag. A factory Trans-Am Javelin will have a Matador Red engine compartment, a Frost White midsection and a Commodore Blue tail section. When the dealers created a Trans-Am replica, they generally started with a factory-white car; few if any would have received a repaint of the engine compartment to red.

⬇ All of the 1970 red, white, and blue AMC Trans Am Javelins were powered by a 390-cubic-inch V-8 that produced 325 horsepower.

← This AMC Trans Am Javelin is equipped with modern Goodyear Eagle GT radial tires. The original fitment from the factory was F70×14 Goodyear Polyglas tires.

← The 1970 Javelin dash was dramatically changed over the previous year's appearance. Although it shared most components with the 1970 AMX, the woodgrain overlay and steering wheel center called out the Javelin name and bull's-eye emblem.

↓ American Motors produced only one hundred of the 1970 Trans-Am Javelin package cars to commemorate a successful 1969 season. All were identically equipped and priced right at $4,000 as seen in this window sticker.

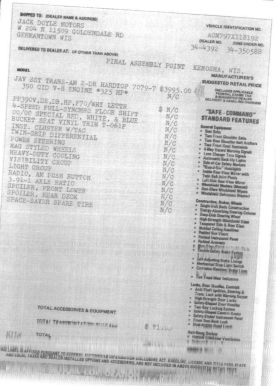

Javelin Mark Donohue Special

THE KAPLAN TEAM had competed with the bigger Chevrolet- and Ford-backed racing teams for two seasons. One consistent issue that prevented victory for the team and season was Roger Penske's Z/28 Camaro team piloted by Mark Donohue. Faced with a competitive situation, the easiest way to both hurt Chevrolet and assist AMC was to steal away the former's team and driver. There has been much speculation as to why Roger Penske chose to switch allegiance for the 1970 season, but the end result brought victories to AMC and Mark Donohue. The Penske team had complete control over the program, without the typical management oversight that had interfered in the past. Donohue needed to get the Javelins to handle better than previous years, and he detected that there was too much flex in the full unibody chassis design used for the production Javelin. He took delivery of brand-new bodies in white and put them through a stiffening and double welding procedure for a more rigid platform.

The previous trunnion design had already been replaced by Kaplan racing with a more typical front upper A-arm design for racing. AMC made this change to all Javelins and AMXs for the 1970 production year. During preliminary testing, Donohue identified inadequate rear downforce at speed and helped to design an oversized ducktail spoiler to assist in this area. To homologate the Javelin for the 1970 season, AMC had to sell a minimum of 2,500 units to the public to qualify any changes for the Trans-Am series. From this requirement, AMC decided to build the Mark Donohue Special Javelin for the 1970 season. It was first introduced in February 1970, and the last factory-built car was produced in April. The Mark Donohue Special was based on the high-end Javelin SST and required one of two top-performance motors. They all came with a 360 four-barrel V-8 (P in the VIN) or 390 four-barrel V-8 (X in the VIN). It was also rumored that some of the 360 engines came with thick web blocks to accommodate a modification for a four-bolt main cap, though this may have been a story to justify differences in the special 304-cubic-inch engines used in the actual 1970 Trans-Am Donohue race cars.

Here are a few things to look for to determine whether a Javelin came from the factory as a Mark Donohue Special: The car must have been built between late January and April 1970. It must be an SST with power front disc brakes and power steering. It can be equipped with the three-speed automatic on the column, a floor-shift auto, or a four-speed on the floor. It must be equipped with a ram-air AMX-style hood with the Javelin emblem on the front of the driver's side. All cars will be equipped with a 360 or 390 four-barrel V-8.

When the Mark Donohue edition was first introduced, the first examples were used by Sunoco, which was a major sponsor of the Penske team. They were driven by women referred to as "Javelin Girls," whose responsibility it was to set up a Sunoco Javelin Trans-Am display in each Sunoco station's front window in their designated area. Each of these Mark Donohue Javelins was equipped the same in a Commodore Blue exterior and a blue vinyl interior with a contrasting white C-stripe. Power was by the tamer of the two engine options, with the 360 V-8 mated to a three-speed automatic transmission.

↑↑ The Mark Donohue Javelins used the AMX ram air hood design to increase performance. This car also has the optional 15x7 Machine wheels that became optional after January 1970. ↑ All Mark Donohue editions were manufactured between late January and mid-April 1970. A total of 2,501 were assembled to meet Trans Am homologation rules for 1970. ←← There was only one advertisement created for the Mark Donohue Specials. Only the spoiler was unique to this model, but certain options were included on each factory car created.

⬆ This profile accentuates the short 97-inch wheelbase that the first generation AMX used. By comparison, the 1970 Corvette wheelbase was 1 inch longer.

THE AMX (American Motors eXperimental) was an anomaly in the muscle-car market. Released four months after the new Javelin in 1968, the AMX looked similar to the Javelin but had a wheelbase 12 inches shorter with specific design details to distinguish it. It had no rear seat but otherwise shared major components with the Javelin—including all structural, suspension, and drivetrain components—as well as other AMC offerings. Most sheet metal was identical except for the rear quarter panels, hood, and grille. This allowed AMC to capitalize on tooling and manufacturing costs across the Javelin line. The expectation was to sell ten thousand two-seat AMXs per year alongside an additional hundred thousand Javelin pony cars created on the same assembly line. Unfortunately the production of the AMX two-seater failed to reach expectations, with just 19,134 total buyers over three years (1968–1970) selecting the only two-seat American-built sports car beside the Corvette.

The AMX was not a practical car, especially for the smallest of the Detroit auto manufacturers. Was it a direct competitor to the fiberglass-body Corvette or more of a pony car than a muscle car? It easily fell into each of these niche markets, and even AMC wasn't clear with its advertising. The first advertisement in 1968 referred to it as a sports car and a future collectible. A later ad in 1969 showed a direct comparison between it, a twelve-year-old Corvette, and an early two-passenger 1957 Thunderbird. The larger four-passenger Javelin was being compared to the Mustang in corresponding advertisements, but the AMX didn't have a direct competitor in 1968, especially with its base price of $3,300. (It should be noted that most AMXs came heavily optioned and were closer to the $4,000 mark when new.)

By the third and final model year of the two-seat sports car, the AMX had put on some muscles. Gone was the base 290-cubic-inch engine, replaced by either the 290-horsepower, 360-cubic-inch V-8 or the "AMX" 390-cubic-inch V-8 producing 325 horsepower. Additionally the AMX's look changed for 1970, with a bulging ram air scoop and flush front grille giving the appearance of a longer and wider engine compartment. The improved muscular look fits more into the appearance of a 1970 Mustang Mach 1 or 'Cuda with their shaker hood-scoop option, distinct from the previous AMX.

The new hood and grille design added 2 inches overall, but otherwise the car shared the same sheet metal as the previous two years of AMX production. The rear-end appearance was also updated giving a wall-to-wall taillight look without requiring any costly changes to the quarter panel, trunk lid, or rear bumper.

Even with the improved appearance and performance, the 1970 AMX failed to secure a future two-seat version. AMC had failed to meet its goal of producing ten thousand AMXs per year, and the experiment was about to come to an end. With only 4,116 sold that year, AMC would decide to turn the AMX into a performance option package for the four-seat 1971 Javelin. (One two-seat prototype, with the new Javelin front clip grafted on to a 1970 AMX, was produced and was Dick Teague's personal car.) This decision ended the classification issue—was it a sports car or pony car?—bringing the Javelin AMX into the pony-car class for its final four years of production. As a side note, AMC introduced the 401-cubic-inch engine for 1971 and was the only muscle-car manufacturer that had both a size and horsepower increase for the 1971 model year.

☛ AMC provided several go-fast options under its Group 19 accessory program. This 1970 AMX has the Edelbrock STR-11 cross-ram manifold that was available over the counter at AMC dealerships.

⬇ Most AMXs were equipped with 14-inch Magnum 500 wheels that limited tire size. This owner has chosen to add larger 15-inch wheels while keeping the traditional look of the Magnum 500 design.

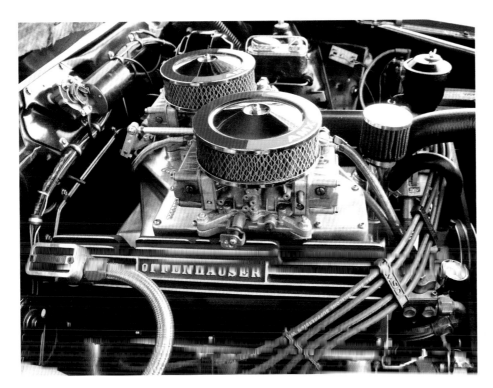

Epilogue

THE MUSCLE CAR, 50 YEARS LATER

By 1974 the first muscle-car era had essentially ended. Ever-encroaching emission, fuel-economy, and safety standards required the manufacturers to dedicate scarce engineering resources to meet these needs. The insurance industry, targeting inexperienced young drivers and high-performance cars, had a corresponding impact. The 1973 Yom Kippur War, which led to the first OPEC oil embargo, was the final nail in the original muscle car's coffin.

Even the biggest engines, struggling under reduced compression ratios requiring low-lead and then no-lead fuels to meet Corporate Average Fuel Economy (CAFE) standards, struggled to produce 200 horsepower. It was the worst of times for enthusiasts who defined performance by speed.

Post-1974 might best be characterized as an era of scoops, stripes, and spoilers, when graphics and adornments compensated for the absence of the high-compression engines that had produced the ground-pounding torque of the previous decade.

To confuse matters further, 1971 marked the transition from gross to net horsepower ratings, with many US manufacturers listing both. A complete changeover was instituted in 1972. California law required that new cars sold in that state advertise only the more conservative net measurement beginning with the 1972 model year. The gross figure rated the engine only, measured on an engine stand; the net rating measured it with all accessories and components (alternator, power steering pump, etc.) attached.

The real decline started in 1972 with the full transition to net ratings and the reduction of compression ratios across the board to accommodate low-lead fuels required of catalytic converters. (Reverse effects also apply; modern fuels are hard on vintage engines, which require hardened valve seats when rebuilt to run on lead-free gas.)

Performance would slowly return, driven by technology advances that allowed new performance without significant negative impacts on emissions and fuel economy. These developments were able to keep the stoichiometric air-to-fuel ratio of 14.7:1. In the world of carburetors we would strive to meet this ideal number, but in reality we often overfueled the car in the process, producing massive and dangerous emissions. With the combination of modern fuel injection, multiple oxygen sensors, variable timing, and computer controls, high-horsepower engines can now be comfortably driven with air-conditioning and all modern conveniences.

⬆ Today's muscle car enthusiast has become familiar with the Challenger's high-performance options. Names like Hellcat, Demon, and widebody are synonymous with discussions about Dodge's current offerings.

⬆ There was a period of time in the 1980s when many thought muscle cars were dead. The Buick GSX turbocharged V-6 offerings held the king-of-the-hill title for many years.

⬆ Today's Camaro has more power and handling capabilities than most previous generations of the Corvette.

GENERAL MOTORS

In 1974 Ford introduced the downsized Mustang II, leaving the Chevrolet Camaro and Pontiac Firebird to soldier on with basically the same car introduced in the strike-shortened 1970 model year. Both would go a decade before they were replaced with third-generation models in 1982. (The AMC Javelin was also discontinued in 1974.)

The one muscle-car outlier during the 1980s was Buick's Regal-based Grand National, introduced for the 1984 model year, which featured a 200-horsepower turbocharged 3.8-liter V-6. It came of age in 1987 with the turbocharged, intercooled, 235-horsepower V-6, and rivaled the Corvette as America's fastest production car.

In 1993 the Camaro and Firebird reached their third generation, which would run for almost a decade. Several performance models were offered: Z/28 and IROC for Camaro and the Trans Am for Pontiac. In 2002 the long-lived F-body platform was discontinued, a victim of changing consumer tastes.

Camaro would return to the Chevrolet lineup for the 2010 model year. The new take on an old theme was based on a variation of the Holden (Australia-built) rear-wheel-drive Zeta platform. Unfortunately, just as the Camaro was reintroduced, GM filed for bankruptcy and shut down the Pontiac division in the aftermath of the 2008 economic meltdown. The event placed a tombstone on the Firebird/Trans Am line, though it didn't stop some clever aftermarket manufacturers from tooling up Firebird-style body kits for the Camaro.

Throughout the following decade, the Camaro was continually improved. For 2020 Chevrolet offered the 650-horsepower supercharged ZL1. It delivers 11.4-second quarter-mile passes all day long with a full factory warranty. And on the drive home, equipped with either a six-speed manual gearbox or a ten-speed automatic transmission, the ZL1 returns 20 miles per gallon in regular freeway driving. All this has a starting price at $65,000—the equivalent of $9,800 in 1970, or almost twice the cost of a Chevelle SS454 LS6 during that era.

But Camaro's future is uncertain. Rumors have surfaced that Camaro production would end for a second time around 2023 as GM continues to focus resources on trucks, crossovers, and SUVs. If Camaro fades away, Chevrolet's performance banner will be carried solely by the Corvette.

FORD

In 1979 Ford introduced the rear-wheel-drive Fox-platform Mustang, marking a new era at Ford and setting the stage for a long road back to muscle-car respectability. The automaker dusted off some storied Shelby nameplates for its highest-performance Mustangs in the years that followed. Since the introduction of the current generation, Mustang sales have declined every year, from 105,932 in 2016 to 72,489 for 2019, when it was outsold for the first time by the Dodge Challenger.

The Mustang brand represents huge equity for Ford Motor Company, and in the 2021 model year was the company's only remaining passenger-car nameplate. In 2020 Ford announced plans to expand to its first full battery-electric vehicle, the Mustang Mach-E. With its full-electric drivetrain, it will be among the fastest Mustangs ever produced and provide the bridge to Ford's electric future.

The Mach-E resembles a Ford Edge more than a Mustang pony car, although both the front fascia and rear taillights create a direct connection to the first- and sixth-generation Mustangs. Ford claims that the all-electric four-door vehicle will have a two motor options, with the top-spec version offering the equivalent of 459 horsepower. It has a promised range of 300 miles.

Performance is anticipated to be 0 to 60 in 3.5 seconds and an estimated quarter-mile time of less than 14 seconds. (As a point of reference, the $100,000 Tesla Model S can complete the quarter mile in an impressive 10.6 seconds at 127.55 miles per hour.) Basic models will start at $45,000 with a Mach-E GT Performance Edition starting at around $60,000. With the current battery recharge cost at about one-third the cost of gasoline, the performance per dollar ratio may finally encourage traditional enthusiasts to go electric.

⬆ The future of the Mustang is electric, as seen here with the 2021 Mustang Mach-E. It combines the sportiness of a traditional Mustang, the utility of an SUV such as the Explorer, and the acceleration of Ford's own third-generation GT supercar.

🐎 After producing the Pinto-based Mustang II, Ford returned to producing a larger Mustang for the 1979 model year. Over the subsequent decade, the Fox platform Mustang offered both a turbocharged four-cylinder model as well as ever more powerful V-8 engines.

🐎 Until the arrival of the Mach-E, Ford will continue to offer traditional high-performance, V-8-powered, rear-wheel-drive Mustangs well into the mid-2020s.

CHRYSLER

Chrysler and Dodge stepped up performance in 2005 with the four-door 300, the short-lived Magnum station wagon, and the Charger—all powered by a third-generation Hemi V-8 and available in high-performance SRT versions. In spring 2008, Dodge took the wraps off the Challenger SRT8, followed in 2009 by a full range of two-door Challengers based on the same rear-wheel-drive LX platform that underpinned the 300, Magnum, and Charger.

Over the next decade, like Ford, Dodge introduced more powerful Challengers, such as the Hellcat and Demon. The 2018-only Demon was offered with a supercharged 808-horsepower V-8.

There is a great deal of speculation as to what will come of Chrysler's rear-wheel-drive performance cars, especially in advance of its merger with PSA. The second-generation Challenger saw its best sales ever in 2019: 81,514 worldwide, surpassing even the 76,935 Challengers Dodge sold in 1970, its initial year.

With Charger sales remaining healthy at 100,360 for 2019, observers await all-new models for 2023. Initially it was thought that both the Charger and Challenger would be based on the Giorgio platform that underpins the Alfa Romeo Giulia, but those rumors have been quashed. Instead the new models are expected to be extensively revised platforms of the current Chargers and Challengers, each put on strict weight-saving diets of at least 500 pounds.

THE FUTURE

The future of the muscle car will certainly be electric. This transition will take time, but the torque available from electric powertrains offers potential performance that we could only have dreamed of even during the pinnacle of the muscle car's first Golden Age in 1970.

Back then, a truly quick big-block muscle car would take all of a driver's skill to break the 6-second mark from 0 to 60. Today's quickest vehicles can do it in less than half that time. And the quarter mile? The Challenger Hellcat Demon can rip off 1,320 feet in just 9.65 seconds at 152 miles per hour on skinny front tires and 100-octane race fuel. That's mighty fast for a car that you can drive to the track and back home with the air-conditioning on.

For those who came of age in the 1960s and 1970s, driving is a visceral experience. It's all about the tactile. It's the road feel transmitted to your left hand gripping the thin-rimmed, oversized plastic steering wheel, feedback coming from the four tiny patches of rubber connecting car to pavement. It's the windows rolled down, with the once state-of-the-art factory-installed eight-track player sending Chicago's "25 or 6 to 4" to four low-fidelity, whizzer-cone speakers while your right hand grips the ball of the Hurst shifter.

That spirit is not gone. We think about progress as we look to the future. And despite periodic efforts to legislate performance cars out of existence, we believe the best is yet to come.

← If any company has been successful in the modern muscle car category, it's FCA, who has kept its Dodge Challenger platform fresh with many models and performance packages. Its Hellcat-powered models bring 200 miles per hour within reach of the masses.

⬇ One of the models that keeps the Dodge Challenger relevant is its widebody version. Shown here on the Challenger, the widebody package is also offered on its Charger models, making it a four-door muscle car.

Acknowledgments

THIS BOOK WAS COMPLETED under very difficult conditions. Just as we made preparations to finish the text and get the final photos, the COVID-19 pandemic hit. This really impacted our ability to acquire the remaining photos, a list that included about a dozen cars. We planned to spend the spring of 2020 photographing the remaining vehicles, finish up the text, and captioning the images. With the COVID lockdowns, that plan was thrown to the wind.

Thankfully we both have extensive social media presences that we employed to acquire many of the needed photographs. Mostly connecting with marque-specific car interest groups on Facebook and through other social media platforms like Flickr, we were able to find almost all the missing photographs.

Often owners already had publication-quality photographs they could submit. But in other instances, we were able to walk them through the process of shooting publication-quality photographs for *1970 Maximum Muscle*. All we can say is thank God for digital cameras and, in some cases, smartphones that are capable of producing outstanding images. These contributors include Joy Curran, Paul Gold, Dave Klemenz, Jameson Leavell, Robert Leenstra, William Moglia, Rick Rittenberg, Alisha Seigworth, Ed Stone, Ben Virga, Cindy Walden, James Wilson, and Mark Winkelman.

Because of the crush that always accompanies the completion of any book, especially one finished during an unprecedented national lockdown, if we missed mentioning you and your contributions, please accept our apologies. Let us know so you can be recognized in future printings. And, of course, there's our longtime colleague Steve Statham, the former editor of *Musclecar Enthusiast* and the author of several muscle car books at Motorbooks, who was invaluable in putting together this book.

One group of contributors that we would like to call out in particular includes Edd Dedick, Andrew Mackey, and owner Mark Pieloch of the American Muscle Car Museum in Melbourne, Florida. The collection was a virtual treasure trove of cars, and they provided images that were used to fill out the final list of missing cars, particularly several in the Ford chapter. We really appreciate their contributions.

Finally, we would like to mention two friends who contributed to *1970 Maximum Muscle* but unfortunately will not see its publication, Arnold Marks and Dave Lindsley. Both passed away while we were producing this book.

We first met Arnold and his wife Jan on our 2006 feature "Muscle Cars on the Mother Road." Arnold, well known in both prewar and postwar vintage car circles, was the owner of Mustangs, Etc. In Van Nuys, California. Arnold had already forgotten more about classic Mustangs than we will ever know.

And then there's Dave Lindsley. Dave, like Arnold, was a consummate car guy. Dave had a small but spectacular multi-marque muscle car collection that was always changing. He had a 1967 Plymouth GTX Hemi that made it into several magazines, but his passions were always centered around Chevys. One of the centerpieces of his collection was his 1969 Camaro Z/28, which leads off the Trans Am section of our book.

We both learned a lot about muscle cars from Dave. As we finished this book in the summer of 2020, we often felt Dave looking over our shoulders. We both feel sad that having helped us in so many ways over the years, he didn't live long enough to see this book's completion. But we agree that Arnold and Dave will have smiles on their faces in muscle car heaven when *1970 Maximum Muscle* reaches bookstores.

Mark Fletcher
Richard Truesdell
November 2020

Image Credits

A = all, B = bottom, C = center, L = left, R = right, T = top

All photography by Richard Truesdell except:

Michael Conrad: 75BL, 75BR. **Tim Costello:** 14TR, 24 –25A. **Ed Dedick/ Andrew Mackey/American Muscle Car Museum:** 55A, 84BR, 88–90A, 102 –103A. **FCA:** 10R, 17B, 166L, 170, 171. **Ford Media:** 11, 87, 104, 168A, 169. **Getty Images:** 6R (Bettmann). **GM Heritage Center:** 75T. **GM Media Archives:** 10L, 11, 114T, 129, 167. **Paul Gold:** 97T. **Chad Horwedel:** 23. **Don Keefe:** 126–128A. **Jameson Leavell/Fast Lane Classic Cars:** 80 –83A, 150–151A. **Robert Leenstra:** 140. NASA: 6L. **David Newhardt/Mecum Auctions:** 166R. **Public Domain:** 8L, 8R. **Wayne Schmeeckle:** 97B. **Lon Seigworth:** 22. **Jordan Sneathen:** 84TR, 84CR, 98–101A. **Steve Statham:** 46CR, 48 –53A. **Bryan Tyner/KC Classic Auto:** 78–79A. **Ben Virga:** 120–121A. **Cindy Walden/ECS Automotive Concepts:** 138–139A.

Index

Inspiring | Educating | Creating | Entertaining

Brimming with creative inspiration, how-to projects, and useful information to enrich your everyday life, Quarto Knows is a favorite destination for those pursuing their interests and passions. Visit our site and dig deeper with our books into your area of interest: Quarto Creates, Quarto Cooks, Quarto Homes, Quarto Lives, Quarto Drives, Quarto Explores, Quarto Gifts, or Quarto Kids.

© 2021 Quarto Publishing Group USA Inc.
Text © 2021 Mark Fletcher and Richard Truesdell

First Published in 2021 by Motorbooks, an imprint of The Quarto Group, 100 Cummings Center, Suite 265-D, Beverly, MA 01915, USA. T (978) 282-9590 F (978) 283-2742 QuartoKnows.com

All rights reserved. No part of this book may be reproduced in any form without written permission of the copyright owners. All images in this book have been reproduced with the knowledge and prior consent of the artists concerned, and no responsibility is accepted by producer, publisher, or printer for any infringement of copyright or otherwise, arising from the contents of this publication. Every effort has been made to ensure that credits accurately comply with information supplied. We apologize for any inaccuracies that may have occurred and will resolve inaccurate or missing information in a subsequent reprinting of the book.

Motorbooks titles are also available at discount for retail, wholesale, promotional, and bulk purchase. For details, contact the Special Sales Manager by email at specialsales@quarto.com or by mail at The Quarto Group, Attn: Special Sales Manager, 100 Cummings Center, Suite 265-D, Beverly, MA 01915, USA.

24 23 22 21 20   1 2 3 4 5

ISBN: 978-0-7603-6678-3

Digital edition published in 2021
eISBN: 978-0-7603-6679-0

Library of Congress Cataloging-in-Publication Data

Names: Fletcher, Mark, 1959- author. | Truesdell, Richard, author.
Title: 1970 maximum muscle : the pinnacle of muscle car power / Mark Fletcher, Richard Truesdell.
Description: Beverly, MA, USA : Motorbooks, an imprint of The Quarto Group, 2021. | Includes index. | Summary: "1970 Maximum Muscle explores the factors that would lead to the decline of the most exciting era in the American automotive industry-as well as the resulting arms race among designers who saw their last opportunity to make the ultimate muscle car. As a result, 1970 was the climax of the muscle car era from engineering, styling, and performance standpoints"-- Provided by publisher.
Identifiers: LCCN 2020039714 (print) | LCCN 2020039715 (ebook) | ISBN 9780760366783 (hardcover) | ISBN 9780760366790 (ebook)
Subjects: LCSH: Muscle cars--History. | Automobile industry and trade--United States--History--20th century.
Classification: LCC TL23 .F56 2021 (print) | LCC TL23 (ebook) | DDC 629.222--dc23
LC record available at https://lccn.loc.gov/2020039714
LC ebook record available at https://lccn.loc.gov/2020039715

Acquiring Editor: Dennis Pernu
Cover Images: Rich Truesdell
Design: Cindy Samargia Laun

Printed in China

This publication has not been prepared, approved, or licensed by Ford, General Motors, or FCA.

We recognize, further, that some words, model names, and designations mentioned herein are the property of the trademark holder. We use them for identification purposes only. This is not an official publication.